FINDING GOD IN HARD PLACES

DR. MICHAEL A. BELL

PAST PRESIDENT OF THE BAPTIST GENERAL CONVENTION OF TEXAS

Finding God in Hard Places

©Copyright 2021 by Dr. Michael A. Bell

All rights reserved.

No portion of this book may be reproduced, stored in a retrieval system, or transmitted in any form or by means—electronic, mechanical, photocopy, recording, scanning, or other excerpt for brief quotations in critical reviews or articles, without prior written permission of the publisher.

ISBN: 978-1-955622-74-5

Published by:

Fideli Publishing
119 W Morgan St
Martinsville, IN 46151

www.FideliPublishing.com

Table Of Contents

Introduction..v
1. Turning Back When the Fight Starts.................................1
2. Frustrated Expectations 8
3. On The Horns Of A Dilemma....................................15
4. Living In Time Between..21
5. Discouraged Because Of The Way.............................27
6. Famine In The Land Of Promise...............................33
7. A Place Called Wits' End 40
8. Overwhelmed 45
9. Missing Spain But Getting A Dungeon....................51
10. Making Hay While The Sun Shines 57
11. Fight Instructions...63
12. Fighting Back Against Falling Back..........................68
13. Interruptedpages 73
14. When Things Get So Bad You Want To Clock Out.................79
15. Shattered Dreams...86
16. Limiting God..91
17. God Spoke To Job Out Of The Storm......................97
18. Quitters Don't Win Fights.......................................102
19. Picturing The Possible 106

Introduction

Theodicy [THē ädəsē] is the word used to describe our *(meaning Homo sapiens)* efforts in attempting to answer the question of why painful things happen to good or innocent people. To borrow Rabbi Harold Samuel Kushner's question, "Why do bad things happen to good people?" Immediately, when I think of the theodicy question, my thoughts turn to Sunday, September 15, 1963, when white supremacists bombed the 16th Street Baptist Church in Birmingham, Alabama, killing four African American girls, all under the age of 15, and injuring many more. And who can forget the horrendous Charleston, South Carolina Church massacre on June 17, 2015, in which Dylann Roof, a 21-year-old white supremacist, murdered nine African Americans who were attending Bible study at the Emanuel African Methodist Episcopal Church, located in that county seat city.

Of course, there have been more recent atrocities that we could easily reference because we live in a world where catastrophe is commonplace and the love of God isn't always apparent. The late theologian Gordon D. Kaufman *(born June 22, 1925; died July 22, 2011)* wrote, in his book *God The Problem*, "It is because God is conceived as power *and* goodness, the problem of theodicy is so poignant and difficult." But, my faith supports my conviction that the God Jesus knows and reveals doesn't plot, plan or perpetuate suffering and tragedy. I contend that God takes the rap for a lot of things he never willed should happen and throughout this book I argue that the problem of evil has less to do with God and more to do with what we — as human beings — are willing to allow. In Romans 8:28, the Apostle Paul, the Church's most celebrated preacher, says something truly remarkable: "All things work together for good for those who love God, who are called according to his purpose." This momentous verse expresses that evil and pain is never the will of God, but God can take evil and pain and use it for good.

Finding God in Hard Places is about learning to trust God when your life is unbottomed by devastation and you can't seem to figure out what to do next. Yes, there are some "hard places" in life when we can candidly echo the dying words of Marlon Brando's Colonel Walter Kurtz, in the 1979 movie, *Apocalypse Now*, "the horror, the horror, the horror," but the Bible teaches that *even* in the face of gut-wrenching, soul-horrifying tragedy, we can trust that God can bear the weight of all that we're experiencing.

Dr. Michael A. Bell

CHAPTER ONE

Turning Back When the Fight Starts

⁹The Ephraimites, being armed and carrying bows, turned back in the day of battle. ¹⁰They broke their agreement with God, and refused to live by his instructions. ¹¹They forgot what he had done, and the miracles that he had shown them.

—Psalm 78:9-11, FT

Ephraim was one of the twelve tribes of Israel. The Ephraimites were descendants of Ephraim, one of the two sons of Joseph *(Manasseh being the other)*. The poet of Psalm 78 says that the Ephraimites were "armed and carrying bows." The word translated "carrying" literally means "to hurl or to shoot." The point is that the Ephraimites had the weaponry — the arsenal to fight and they were "shooters of bows," in other words, they were skilled archers — but when the time for fighting came they were nowhere to be found.

What a sad commentary on a people who had been highly favored by God. Rather than driving out the inhabitants of the Promised Land as God had instructed them, they turned back in the day of battle and didn't finish the job of conquering their part of the Promised Land. They were equipped with the finest weapons of the time and they had God's promise of victory to help them drive out the Canaanites and yet they turned back in the day of battle.

When Scripture says here that the Ephraimites "turned back" on God it's not talking about **salvation** — it's talking about **service**. It's not talking about **conversion** — it's talking about **commitment**.

This whole thing of commitment and service is something that the Lord takes very seriously. As a matter of fact, Jesus said that if you put your hand to plow and turn back you aren't even fit for God's Kingdom *(Luke 9:62)*.

The Ephraimites had a promising beginning which led to prosperity and honor. From the tribe of Ephraim came Joshua, Gideon, and Samuel. The tribe of Ephraim had everything that it needed to be successfully used by God. They possessed the skills and weaponry to fight the battle. The Ephraimites had been protected, provided for and blessed by God, and yet there came a point in which they turned back on God.

And this is the first thing I want you to remember: **There is more than the matter of extrinsic appearances in the service of God.** From the outside, everything looked well with Ephraim. They were equipped with the finest weapons of the time and they had

God's promise to help them drive out the Canaanites and yet they turned back in the day of battle.

For me it is easy, painless, and comfortable to confess I believe in God and I follow Jesus, our crucified and resurrected Savior. Like many of you, one of the first Scriptures I was taught after I was saved was Ephesians 2:8: "For by grace are you saved through faith ... ." But what about Ephesians 2:10? "For we are what God has made us, created in Christ Jesus for good works, which God prepared beforehand to be our way of life!"

"The Ephraimites, being armed and carrying bows, turned back in the day of battle."

This is one of the saddest things that I see as a pastor. I mean, in my 49-plus years of ministry I've seen church member after church member after church member who has done the same thing. They get into the heat of the battle, they get into the middle of the fight — then, sooner or later, they begin to face some opposition and they turn tail and run.

Why is that? Why did the Ephraimites turn back, as it says here, "in the day of battle?" Why do Christians today turn back when things get a little hot — when things get a little hard — when things get a little difficult?

Notice the testimony of the text about how God provided for their needs and protected his people from their enemies. Do you remember how God had provided for them there in the wilderness? Do you remember how God gave them Manna and quail every morning for breakfast? Do you remember how God gave them water out of that rock?

Did you catch that? These are just a few examples of how God watches over those who serve him. But not only that, I believe these references serve as a very strong warning to those of us who either have or are considering turning back on God.

I want you to pray that the Holy Spirit would speak to you like he's never spoken before because I believe that it's a very serious thing for you to set out to serve God and then at some point, for some reason turn back on God.

Now, what does that mean to you? Because I don't want you to miss the whole point of why God put this story in the Bible. The Ephraimites' downfall was two-fold. First, **they stopped following God**. Verse ten recounts, "They broke their agreement with God, and refused to live by his instructions."

How did Jesus stay focused on his mission? We believe that it was because of his habits. Habits are behaviors and actions that we often do instinctively, often without much thought. Jesus' habits, his spiritual disciplines, were something that he practiced as a regular part of his daily life.

The habits that Jesus practiced — spending time in solitude and prayer, applying God's word, abiding in God's unconditional love, and maintaining supportive relationships — kept his life and leadership perfectly aligned with God the Father. God uses our habits *(spiritual disciplines)* to put us into a place where God can work within us to transform us into the leaders that God wants us to become.

Practicing these habits align your life with God's will and purposes, keeping you on course much like the alignment of your car's tires keeps your car headed in the right direction. When your car is "out of alignment," the tires or wheels that are not aligned properly will pull or steer the car in a different direction from that of the remaining ones. If you are not careful while you are driving, your car might veer over into another lane or even run off the road into a ditch.

Through our habits, God continually realigns and transforms our life so that our heart, head and hands remain focused on the purpose and mission that God has given to us. Practicing them on a daily basis prevents us from losing our direction and keeps us out of the "ditches" that Satan, culture and the slings and arrows of outrageous fortune put in our way.

When we are out of alignment with God, it hampers our ability to effectively do the work tasked to our hands. We can be crippled for days on end. Our relationship with God is a living, breathing one that needs to be fed, watered and fertilized. When off track, we can course correct and get an alignment or adjustment by simply crying out to God and we can then stay aligned by maintaining constant contact with him.

When we step out of alignment with God's love, his rest, his peace, or even his willingness to provide, our lives can quickly fall into misalignment on all sorts of levels.

Many of us are unaware that our lives are misaligned. We are quick to blame forces outside of ourselves — the circumstances, people, government, and too often, our common adversary — for what isn't working in our lives. But more often, we allow our lives to become misaligned because of socialization. We defer to our relational constellation, the people we hang around, and how we were brought up to determine how high we fly.

Here is a quick litmus test that will tell you if you are in alignment with God: **If you're not growing, your life is out of alignment.**

Once they had stopped following God, the next logical step is to **forget God.** Verse eleven reads, "They forgot what he had done, and the miracles that he had shown them." I don't think the idea of forgetting God means they were like, "God who?" Rather I think it carries with it the idea of taking no thought of God. They forgot God by not considering what he had said when making their decisions. God's will and God's Word had no place in their decision-making process.

If you find yourself being pulled away from your loyalty and devotion to God, it helps to **remember what you're fighting for.** As soldiers of the Cross and followers of Christ, we fight battles on a daily basis. Some are internal, like the fight for personal integrity. Others are on behalf of others, like the fight for equal access and opportunity for our children and to provide for our families.

One more thing. **Remember whose side you're on.** How many times have you heard a sport's team claim the reason for their victory was because "God was on our side?" But the more appropriate question is "Who is fighting on the Lord's side?" As Christ's ambassadors, it should be apparent in our daily choices whose side we're on. Being on the Lord's side is demonstrated by living out the message of the gospel. And that's what God wants ... right? God wants God's people to act out the implications of our theology, to put our faith to work positively and creatively, whatever the circumstances in which we may find ourselves.

Back in the long ago, Moses asked, "Who is on the Lord's side? *(Exodus 32:26)*" Whoever you are, wherever you are on your personal journey, God has high hopes and expectations for the you God intends you to be. Stay in the fight! Remain faithful!

CHAPTER TWO

Frustrated Expectations

¹When Jesus had finished giving these instructions to his twelve disciples, he went out to teach and preach in towns throughout the region. ²John the Baptist, who was in prison, heard about all the things the Messiah was doing. So he sent his disciples to ask Jesus, ³"Are you the Messiah we've been expecting, or should we keep looking for someone else?" ⁴Jesus told them, "Go back to John and tell him what you have heard and seen— ⁵the blind see, the lame walk, those with leprosy are cured, the deaf hear, the dead are raised to life, and the Good News is being preached to the poor." ⁶And he added, "God blesses those who do not fall away because of me."

— Matthew 11:1-6, NLT

Expectations can be risky. We all have great expectations at different times in our lives; expectations of our friendships...jobs...relationships...children...our church membership ... so forth and so on. We also have certain expectations of God and how we expect God to act toward us based upon our knowledge of him. However, serious problems arise when God does not act as we expected him to.

Expectations can be exciting ... and yet disappointing when they don't materialize. What kind of expectations do we have of God? Our expectations can shape our image and idea of God. We see ourselves in a relationship with God, then come with a set of hopes and beliefs. What do we do when our expectations of God are not met? Maybe we should reexamine our expectations or our image of God, or maybe both.

John the Baptist sits in prison incarcerated in a death row dungeon cell, awaiting his fate. Some time has passed since John showed up at the Jordan river, baptizing people with water for repentance and calling out the Sadducees and Pharisees for their hypocrisy. But, now his ax-wielding days are past and the Baptizer is wondering if he got it right when he tagged Jesus as the expected Messiah. Could he have been wrong? His whole life's purpose was to prepare the way for the One who would usher in God's kingdom, and still corrupt King Herod has the power to lock him up for telling the truth, the whole truth and nothing but the truth. Jesus is roaming the Judean countryside teaching and preaching, and Rome still has its boot on the neck of the Israelites. And the so-called religious leaders still live it up in their places of privilege. John is having a crisis of faith. Doubt has replaced certainty; hesitation has replaced boldness. He's second guessing. Is it any wonder that he would ask his disciples, "What's happening with Jesus?"

John anticipated that the Messiah would usher in a season of judgment and divine retribution. But so far nothing like that has happened; in fact it has been quite the opposite. Jesus' ministry has been more about teaching, healing, and compassion than judgment. He has been moving among the people, teaching them about the kingdom of God, healing their diseases, and fellowshipping with the pariahs and misfits of society. He breaks customs and challenges societal norms — but there is no sign of judgment. John was looking for a Judgment-Messiah, and, in his estimation, Jesus isn't living up to the expectations of what a Messiah should be doing. Jesus is falling short of the expectation of being a religious and political figure. The expectation was for a Messiah who would come to restore Israel to its former glory. And, now John the Baptist, the faithful prophet who preached the coming of the Messiah and shouted, "Behold, the Lamb of God" when he first saw Jesus, was doubting as to whether Jesus was the real deal. As a result, he sent his followers to ask Jesus if he had it wrong. "Are you the One, or should we be looking for someone else?"

Have you ever had a moment like that? Where you knew who God is and you knew who Jesus is and you were firm in your faith, but then something hit you that knocked you off balance? Something happened that caused you to question what you thought you really believed, and you weren't sure what to do anymore.

Many of us have stories like John's. You see, unbelief often surfaces because life is not turning out as we had thought, and the result can be a crisis or failure of faith. Disappointing circumstances can create unbelief. Discouragement, a feeling of futility and hopelessness, can cause doubt and unfulfilled expectations. The tension between what we'd hoped for and what we are experiencing can challenge what we believe. The prison bars that hold us don't always give way. Our doubts don't always resolve themselves. Justice doesn't always arrive in time or sometimes not at all. Questions don't always receive the answers we hunger for — and this, too, is what the life of faith looks like. Our faith asks us to not to take offense, to stay with it.

"Are you the one, who is to come? Or are we to look for another?"

But Jesus doesn't give John or us the answer of yes or no we want. He doesn't say, "Yes, I am the Messiah." He doesn't say "Keep looking."

Notice that Jesus' answer to John's disciples was one of hope — and hope is not without questions or doubts. No...Jesus doesn't criticize John for a lack of faith. He understands John's confusion. Jesus doesn't fear the question because he has the answer. He simply responds, "You're focused on the wrong thing. Go back and report to John what you hear and see: The blind receive sight, the lame walk, those who have leprosy are cured, the deaf hear, the dead are raised, and the good news is preached to the poor." Then, he adds, "God blesses those who do not fall away because of me."

Here is what Jesus was saying: "Listen, you just let John know this: Even if you don't understand my method, even if you don't grasp my ways or my timing, I am asking you to trust me. Don't turn away from me, don't doubt what you know to be true because I don't do what you expect me to do! When you are unable to see why I am doing what I am doing, *or* why I am not doing what you think I ought to be doing, hang in there. You know who I am. Trust me even in your current difficult circumstance. Don't fall away because of me. Don't fall away because of the way I operate in your life. I'm going to do some things that that don't fit what you thought was going to happen. But don't fall away, stumble, or lose faith."

That's what it means to fall away. The Greek word is *skándalon*. The picture is of a mouse going up to a mousetrap and triggering that little lever and getting trapped. The little lever was called a *skándalon*, that thing that would trigger a trap. Jesus is saying, in short, "Here's all I'm saying to you: don't get trapped by your questions. Don't let them hem you in."

There's a difference between asking questions of God and questioning God. There's a big difference. Jesus didn't say, "Stop asking questions!" He didn't say, "Get rid of the doubts." He said: "Just don't fall away when you have questions. Don't let them trap you."

I believe the Lord is saying the same thing to us today. Our desire is for God to stop and right the obvious wrongs — to intervene and stop this novel coronavirus or whatever it is that challenges our very existence. We want God to miraculously mend what is broken in our culture, in our families and in our lives. Perhaps we have an unmet need for which we have been praying. The message Jesus is sending us is, "Don't fall away, or don't be offended by me because I'm not doing what you think I should be doing." It is time for us to stand firm in our faith in God's promise "I will never leave you."

In times of difficulty, we must hang on to what we know to be true and not give in to doubt. God is still God, and he is working in ways that we may not yet see, but that does not mean he isn't working. Even though it might appear as if what we've counted on has become unhinged, this is a time to stand firm in the Lord and the power of his might!

Stand firm in your life in the Lord. Standing firm involves trusting God in spite of the optics. Also embrace the sovereignty of God. Become comfortable with the phrase, **"I don't know…but God does."** Assume the posture of a child who doesn't know her parents plans but who trusts their motives. We don't know everything that God is doing in our lives. We don't know why situations happen. And we don't know everything there is to know about all occurrences in our lives. The Apostle Paul shouts in Romans 11:33, "Oh the depth of the riches both of the wisdom and knowledge of God! How unsearchable are his judgments and his ways are past finding out!"

John needed to see Jesus for who he really was, not who he thought Jesus should be. And so do you and I. Your doubts, if left unattended, will stifle your faith. You need to go to Jesus, ask him to show himself to you again, in a new way, and see what he's already done.

Whatever you are going through, no matter how hard it is, regardless of what you see as the potential fallout on earth, stay faithful to Christ! Keep your eyes on Jesus! You will be blessed. I don't have all the answers as to when or how, but I can assure you that God keeps his promises. "Blessed is the man who does not fall away on account of me!"

CHAPTER THREE

On The Horns Of A Dilemma

[21] They said to them, "The LORD look upon you and judge! You have brought us into bad odor with Pharaoh and his officials, and have put a sword in their hand to kill us." [22] Then Moses turned again to the LORD and said, "O LORD, why have you mistreated this people? Why did you ever send me? [23] Since I first came to Pharaoh to speak in your name, he has mistreated this people, and you have done nothing at all to deliver your people."

— Exodus 5:21-23, NRSV

God called Moses from the Medianite countryside to confront Pharaoh and tell him to "Let my people go." Having received his marching orders, Moses goes to Pharaoh and demands that he free the Hebrew slaves. However, Pharaoh, *who wasn't impressed with Moses*, flat out rejects Moses' request to release the people — and set his jaw in opposition to Moses and the exodus of the Hebrews. Pharaoh decided to double down and responds with increased brutally against the Children of Israel ... making the slaves' lives even more unbearable. So, he made the slaves find their own straw to make their bricks. They were beaten and brutally mistreated, and their suffering had never been so great. Consequently, the Jewish foremen complained to Pharaoh — and when they left Pharaoh they did a very natural thing, a very human thing — and met Moses and Aaron — and complained to Moses for bringing this hardship on them, and they said, "You have made us obnoxious to Pharaoh and his officials and have put a sword in their hand to kill us" *(Exodus 5:21, NIV).*

Moses had promised them that the Lord was going to deliver them, and that he was going to confront Pharaoh with this word of deliverance from the Lord. Their hopes had been high, but now what Moses had done really worked against them, so they blamed Moses for all their problems. They suggested that he might do everyone a big favor by going back to wherever he came from. And, a dispirited, discouraged, crestfallen and confused Moses begins to question God's character, God's goodness, God's purposes and God's actions — and blames God for not doing what God said he would do. Moses complains, "Since I first came to Pharaoh to speak in your name, he has mistreated this people, and you have done nothing at all to deliver your people."

Moses was hanging on the horns of a dilemma — driven to a wall — in a tight squeeze — behind the eight ball — between the hammer and the anvil — up a creek without a paddle — in a corner — backed up against the wall — hard pressed — caught between a rock and a hard place ... and **his questions far outnumbered his answers.** No matter how you say it, there is no tougher spot to be in than to be faced with a dilemma where there seems to be no help ... no relief ... and no answers!

And it's true, isn't it, that we often get frustrated when we have more questions than answers? And how often are our questions so deep and pervasive that they make us impotent, drain us of energy, and bring us to a state of passive numbness. Our wills are frozen.

Yes, **so often our questions far outnumber the answers** — and that's okay as long as we don't let our questions turn into doubts — and doubts will cause broken fellowship with God and block your blessings.

I have learned from personal experience that living by faith — trusting God means accepting the limits of revelation and affirming the reality of revelation. We normally put the emphasis on what God has revealed, but it is equally important to affirm what God has kept hidden.

Moses says, in Deuteronomy 29:29 that "The secret things belong to the Lord." There will be things in your life that make no sense to you. They will baffle you. You won't be able to work them out. You might feel like throwing up your hands and saying, "Life makes no sense. It is completely absurd. What's the point? I give up!" **But, when we trust God we have to get comfortable with being uncomfortable, with not knowing everything, with not knowing how God is going to accomplish what needs to be done and not knowing when he will do it.**

I don't know what you're going through in your life right now. You may be going through or have been through a divorce process. You may have lost someone close to your heart. Maybe a friend has betrayed you. You may have lost a job. Someone close to you might have an incurable disease. You may have questions of God. I would encourage you to come to God and ask him those questions. Personally, I've asked God the "how long" question when it comes to racial injustice, color prejudice, and systemic bigotry ... and I'm still waiting for an answer.

Listen, I can guarantee you in the name of Jesus that God is big enough to handle your grievances and your grief. So, go ahead and pursue not the answers, but him — the God of all answers — and then you will receive answers. Pursue not just knowledge, but the God of all knowledge. Pursue not just wisdom, but the God of wisdom. Don't get it twisted. God is big enough to handle your unanswered questions. And, here's the shout, you can use your angst and your apprehensiveness to move toward God, instead of running away from him.

Let's spin it out this way. The greatest faith is not a faith that has all the answers. The greatest faith is a faith that is able to face unanswered questions and still follow after Christ.

Moses was hanging on the horns of a dilemma even though he was following God's instructions. It's obvious from even a casual reading of this passage that Moses is struggling with the apparent failure of God's plan. It's as if Moses is saying to the Lord, "Talk to

Pharaoh you say. And I did. But now everyone hates me and no one is rescued. God, did I get it wrong *or* did you get it wrong?"

What if following God's plan *or* obeying God's instructions results in our being inconvenienced or embarrassed? What if things become harder for us in the short term when we're being obedient?

Has that ever happened to you when you tried to serve the Lord or obey God's calling for your life? Don't assume that encountering difficulties means that you're not in God's will.

When you serve the Lord you will face letdowns, setbacks and shake-ups that make it seem like you're on the wrong path — and when you do ... go to God and cry out to him; take time to talk to God. Listen again to Moses talking to God: "My Lord, why have you brought so much trouble on your people? Why did you send me for this? Ever since I first came to Pharaoh to speak in your name, he has abused this people. And you've done absolutely nothing to rescue your people."

Pour out your heart to him, then. God alone is your place of refuge. God is big enough to handle all your irritations and frustrations of whatever nature. Why do we hold back from crying out to God? Maybe we're worried about offending God. Perhaps we're afraid God is going to be unhappy. But as we open our Bibles, we find that many of God's great people were very honest with God about their reversals, their distresses and struggles.

Here's the thing: **even though it didn't seem to be working out, God was still at work.** He was about to put on a pretty epic show in the land of Egypt that would be undeniable. It would be clear that God was the one doing the rescuing, not Moses. It was going to be awesome, but it was going to be in his timing.

We tend to miss seeing what God is doing, too — especially when we have stuck in our head a particular way in which we think God should be working. We think God missed it, that he's too late. He must not understand what's at stake. How could he not know what's going on? Maybe we are the one who don't know what's going on. **Maybe we are looking at life through our microscopic lens rather than God's wide-angle one.** Because I guarantee you that God has a better perspective than we do.

We have the privilege here of knowing the end of the story. Moses can't see what is to come. This day is a tough one. But we know now and God knew then. The plan wasn't derailed.

Listen! We can live with the questions when we remember who God is. God brought to pass what God had promised. Back in old church we used to sing:

God moves in a mysterious way
His wonders to perform
He plants His footsteps in the sea
And rides upon the storm
Judge not the Lord by feeble sense
But trust Him for His grace
Behind a frowning providence

He hides a smiling face

CHAPTER FOUR

Living In Time Between

²Lord, how long will I call for help and you not listen? I cry out to you, "Violence!" but you don't deliver us. ³Why do you show me injustice and look at anguish so that devastation and violence are before me? ⁴There is strife, and conflict abounds. The Instruction is ineffective. Justice does not endure because the wicked surround the righteous. Justice becomes warped.
— Habakkuk 1:2-4, CEB

Habakkuk is only 3 chapters long so it takes up only a few pages. Habakkuk is writing at a time during the divided kingdom of Israel and he was a prophet to Judah. History tells us that Habakkuk lived in Judah, which was the southern of the two kingdoms of Israel. He lived in days leading up to as painful and destructive a moment as the Children of Israel had ever known. It was about 600 BC and Habakkuk saw people who were mistreating and taking advantage of the disinherited and disadvantaged — the marginalized and genetically unwanted. He saw people who thought that violence was the solution to differences and disagreements; he saw friction in families and chaos and conflict in communities. Injustice was running buck wild as people seemed to do whatever they wanted to do with little to no consequence. But in Habakkuk's mind the worst part about it was that the Lord didn't seem to be doing anything to stop the societal oppression and cultural inequities. It almost seemed like God didn't care. The prophet was troubled by the wickedness he saw in society, and he brought some serious questions before God.

As he looks around at the way the world is — he asks God why he doesn't do something. Listen to the frustration in Habakkuk's voice: "How long, O Lord, must I call for help, but you do not listen? Or cry out to you 'Violence,' but you do not save? Why do you make me look at injustice? Why do you tolerate wrong?" This is a lament, a desperate cry for help in the midst of great trouble and malfeasance. Habakkuk's words are a complaint; he has major issues to take up with God. And I suspect we do as well, if we are honest.

Apparently, Habakkuk had repeatedly called upon God to act, to intervene, to set things right, to just do something. Yet it seemed that God hadn't heard a word he was saying and that God wouldn't act to right the wrongs. Finally, out of a deep sense of frustration and confusion, Habakkuk cries out to God, "How long, O Lord, must I call for your help, but you do not listen?!" In other words, **"Lord, please do something! Please ... act like God!"**

Have you ever felt that way? In the wake of a personal tragedy *or* when you were waiting for some good thing to happen and the only thing that keeps happening is bad stuff? Have you ever just wanted to try to wake God up? **"Come on God, don't you see I'm dying here? Why don't you do something?"**

Question. Why is it we automatically assume, when we have any problem or trouble at all, God has left us and we are now all alone? But just as "easy" doesn't necessarily indicate God's presence, neither does difficulty suggest his absence.

Our knee-jerk reaction to trouble — a flat tire, loss of a job, sickness, death, loss of money or material possessions, a tornado or hurricane — is usually to ask, "Has God left me?"

Well, having issued his challenge to God, Habakkuk decides to climb up to a high place, we're told — a place to wait for God's answer. Look at chapter 2, verse 1, "I will keep watch to see what he will say to me," Habakkuk says, "and what he will answer concerning my complaint…"

God's promise had been made — it just hadn't been fulfilled. The promise of peace, the promise of prosperity, the promise of the kingdom of God. Habakkuk had heard it, but had not yet seen it and was still waiting for the fulfillment.

We all want good things to happen in our lives, but too often we want it now ... not later. When it doesn't happen that way, we are tempted to ask, "When, God, when?"

You know ... the truth of the matter is, sometimes there's a long time between vision and fulfillment, isn't there? Sometimes there's a long time between a dream and its realization. We call it the "in-between time." The in-between time is a difficult time between the promise claimed and the promised confirmed. We know God can, but he hasn't yet.

Most of life is lived in the in-between times. In fact, if we think of it, these common moments are the very essence of life. Author and professor, Karoline Lewis says, "We live in, exist in, this constant state of in-betweenness, don't we? The certainness of death but also how to live the most of life here and now ... " Betweenness, transition and change ... these seem to be characteristic of the age we live in.

Times of between show us very clearly what is not God. Who then is God? And where is God at work in these times of between?

Our country is going through an in-between time, too. The economic slide in communities of color. We feel vulnerable and hesitant in ways we've never felt before. We're living in the in-between time. The seemingly never-ending debate about health care reform continues to drag on. We're in the in-between time.

So, how do we live here, where we are? **What can we learn from Habakkuk in the in-between moments of our lives, in the in-between time?**

Now, I don't know about you, but I find it significant that **when Habakkuk hits hard times, the first place he goes is to God.** Did you notice that? This is not the story of somebody who hits a rough patch and gives up on God. No, Habakkuk doesn't quit believing — he doesn't quit practicing his faith. Rather, he goes straight to God and demands an answer to the pain and suffering around him. And God does answer in chapter 2, verses 2-3, "Then the Lord answered me and said, Write a vision, and make it plain upon a tablet so that a runner can read it. There is still a vision for the appointed time; it testifies to the end; it does not deceive. If it delays, wait for it; for it is surely coming; it will not be late."

Habakkuk did not turn away from God because God had never turned away from him. God does not abandon us, even though we can't always see or feel him with us. That's the promise of however many millennia of human history. When Jesus came to the end of his life, just before he ascended to be with his Heavenly Father, he made a promise to his disciples. He did not say, "I'm going to keep you from trouble." He said, instead, "Lo, I am with you always, even unto the and of the age." His promise was of a presence, and that promise has been and will always be enough for us. I choose to believe that!

But there's another part of God's answer to how we live in the meantime — the time between the promise of God and its fulfillment. It's the implied part — the part that gives us confidence when the day is dark. Being "the righteous who live by faith" *(v. 2:4)* does not mean (and has never meant) passivity. People like Habakkuk — people who have "impatiently learned to be patient" — did so by doing something — small things, often — doing things to keep the vision of a better day alive.

God says, the righteous are people who live by faith. And faith is not just a matter of the head, but one of the heart. It is trust. It is dependence on God rather than in ourselves, and as such it is an antidote to pride. That's the more direct answer from God, here. "Don't be boasting in your own strength when things are hard, Habakkuk. Learn to depend on me." And that's not easy, living like that — living by faith. Living by faith means we live with uncertainty. Living by faith means we can live secure in the knowledge that we may have absolute trust, complete confidence, in the promises of God. Now, that doesn't mean that we won't encounter hard knocks in our lives. It doesn't mean that we won't struggle and go through dark nights of the soul. It doesn't mean that we are always bubbling over with joy because we're filled with the Holy Spirit. The difference is that for people of faith the promises of God are always there to ground us. Amen and hallelujah!

CHAPTER FIVE

Discouraged Because Of The Way

⁴ From Mount Hor they set out by the way to the Red Sea, to go around the land of Edom; but the people became very discouraged because of the way. ⁵ The people spoke against God and against Moses, "Why have you brought us up out of Egypt to die in the wilderness? For there is no food and no water, and we detest this miserable food."

— Numbers 21:4-5, NKJV

This is one of those Bible texts that we can all relate to. All of us have it in us to be discouraged when things don't go our way. When we work hard but then don't see the wished-for results, we sometimes become discouraged. Discouragement is one of those potholes on our journey we all hit from time to time.

Discouragement is a feeling of despair — a state of being distraught and distressed *with* a loss of sense or enthusiasm, drive or courage. Discouragement is never the first step in a crisis or negative situation. It's the aftermath of a disappointing or unchanging problem or relationship. Discouragement is the cumulative effect of other things that have gone wrong. We become discouraged either when we don't meet our own expectations *or* when life doesn't meet our expectations ... *or* when others don't meet our expectations, or when God doesn't meet our expectations.

When we get discouraged our attitude and emotions turn negative. When we are discouraged, we don't function in the Spirit realm the way God wants us to. Every one of us has known at one time or another the slap of setback. Life pulls the rug right from under you, and you have nothing to hold on to. Your confidence is shattered. When you're discouraged, you're running low on enthusiasm. Your fighting spirit is weakened and with each successive blow you find yourself less able to pick yourself up and make a new start. For some people, prolonged discouragement leads into depression, a **"What's the use?"** attitude. It causes us to wonder "What's the point in trying?"

Somehow we may think that discouragement hits us only when we don't have our lives together but many people of faith, including some of the greatest saints, have struggled with discouragement. Hannah, Moses, Elijah, Naomi, Jeremiah, Jonah, David, Simon Peter, and other Biblical sheroes and heroes experienced bouts of discouragement. It's a common experience.

One of the most difficult things in life is to stay encouraged. Like rapper Juice World says, "Life's a mess!" And frankly, it's easy to get bogged down in all the turmoil, injustice, and evil that envelop us. There is so much craziness around us from all different sources, right? There's the political sphere, social unrest, injustice, the craziness that goes on on social media that seems to just stir the pot and make matters even worse in some cases.

Please allow me to tell you why discouragement is such a stifling scourge. I've already mentioned that it's a **common experience**. That's number one. Number two is that discouragement is **recurring**. It's not a one-and-done emotion. Experiencing it once doesn't make you immune to getting it again. Discouragement is common to all — it's recurring — and it's contagious. You can catch it from discouraging people.

The opening three verses of Numbers 21 report that the Children of Israel experienced a God-given victory over the king of Arad, and they called the place Mount Hormah, the mountain of destruction. It was their first victory over the inhabitants of the Promised Land. The country of Edom was the last hindrance for them to conquer. They were finally ready to possess their possessions. Moses sent a message to the king of Edom. He asked for a passage through their territory but the Edomites refused them passage. And, consequently, they were told that they would have to reach their goal by taking the long way around. In fact, to go around the Edomites, they had to turn back towards the wilderness and away from Canaan. This was obviously discouraging. And the long way around was not the road of the least resistance. Consequently, the people became discouraged because of the way ... because of the difficulties ... because of the complications ... because of the hardships. In Hebrew, the word "discouraged" means to cut down to size, to diminish hope or to reduce your dreams.

How do we respond when we are discouraged? When nothing seems to be going right it can be easy to become resigned — to feel defeated and hopeless. Although it's impossible to live in an atmosphere totally divorced from discouragement, there are a few positive steps that can be taken to help us be victorious while discouragement surrounds us. Here's a formula for conquering discouragement.

First, **add up all your successes of the past.** Too many times when we're discouraged, we forget our past victories. We so easily forget what God has done for us and the good things that have come our way. Think, for instance, how many times you have barely escaped having an automobile accident. You know that if you had been there one split second sooner, the other car would have hit you. When you drove away, you may have said, "Thank you, Lord, for sparing my life."

Add up all of your past successes. Then, **look for another way forward.** Discouragement generally occurs when our expectations (what we think should happen) don't align with reality (what actually happens). And, when you get discouraged, it doesn't necessarily mean you're doing the wrong thing; you can be doing the right thing in the wrong way.

When you get discouraged, don't dwell on what went wrong. Instead, focus on what to do next. Devise a new approach; try a new attitude. Look to see where you can do better next time, where can you tweak things so you get different results. Look at what you need to stop and take action to eliminate it. What isn't working for you? Maybe you need to stop over thinking or worrying about everything. Maybe you need to stop delaying the risk and go for it. Maybe you need to stop procrastinating. Maybe you need to stop living someone else's life and start becoming the person you are meant to be.

Asking "What can this become?" accelerates you to the kind of fresh vision that fuels your forward motion. Asking what things can become gives you hope and a future!

Look for another way forward — and **pray for discernment.** Brainstorm your options, ideas and possibilities. You can convert your minuses into pluses ... you can transform your difficulties into doors of opportunities ... you can turn your negatives into positives. Dr. Alfred Adler (born February 7, 1870–died May 28, 1937), the famous psychiatrist, claims that one of the most wonderful things about human beings is our capacity to turn reverses into advances.

Look for another way forward. Pray for discernment. Third, remember who God is. Shift your focus from your discouraging circumstances to God. Yes, people do disappoint and hurt us, and we don't always understand God or God's ways. The prophet Nahum talks about a day of trouble and reminds us "The Lord is good, a stronghold in the day of trouble, he knows those who trust in him" *(Nahum 1:7)*. If we're not in close trusting relationship with God, life's discouragements can become unbearable.

Finally, choose to respond to God in praise. If you are feeling discouraged, pray in confidence for God to remove those feelings and begin to praise God for his love and care. This is probably the last thing we want to do when things are going badly for us! But we need to hold on to the truth that, despite our changing circumstances, God never changes! God is faithful to turn desperation into hope - weakness into strength — defeat into victory! God is greater than our grasp of him. God is worthy of our praise!

CHAPTER SIX

Famine In The Land Of Promise

"Now there was a famine in the land, besides the previous famine that had occurred in the days of Abraham ... "
— Genesis 26:1, NASB

A few chapters prior to Genesis 26 ... God called Abraham out of Ur of the Chaldees and promised to give him a land to live in. God promised to bless him and use him to bless others ... and he promised to make Abraham's descendants as numerous as the stars starting with a promised son that Abraham and his wife Sarah had to wait for decades to be born.

Isaac is that promised child, and he is next in the lineage of Abraham. He has inherited all the promises and blessings made to his dad, Abraham. At the time of our text, Isaac, the promised child, the blessed one, the inheritor of the promises ... has been facing a parade of obstacles, disruptions and interruptions, and they seemed to just keep coming.

Genesis 26 opens with a disastrous announcement: "Now there was a famine in the land, besides the previous famine that had occurred in the days of Abraham" *(26:1a)*. The scriptures tell us that the Promised Land was full of famine, drought, and desolation. Famine is the opposite of abundance. Famine means starvation — deprivation — a severe, eviscerating shortage — people in need and in want. Famine is lack — insufficiency — squalor — hardship and distress.

A physical famine is a time when there is no food for the people. Famines throughout history have taken the lives of untold millions. When a famine comes, bodies dry up. Body fat is depleted. Limbs shrivel and people become walking skeletons. Stomachs swell. Faces take on that familiar hollow expression. Disease runs rampant as immune systems are compromised and sanitation systems are overwhelmed.

When we talk about famine as it appears in Scripture, it has to do with the removal of people's potential for fruitfulness, the drying up of their provision, and every order of discomfort and problem that can bring immense pressures to bear.

There was a famine in the land and this was a serious problem for Isaac. The fact that there was a famine, in and of itself, is not unusual. But **the timing of this famine is meant to catch our attention.**

There was a famine in the land and Isaac was in danger of losing everything he had. And, don't miss this ... this famine happened in the "Promised Land," the land God promised Abraham's descendants. Even though Isaac's life was singled out by God for blessing, and even though he's in the center of God's will, he has to deal with a famine. What a reminder that we can be in the "Promised Land" — we can be in the place of blessing, and still experience hardship. We can be where God wants us to be, doing what God wants us to do and still we have to cope with life in all of its suffering and angst.

Yes ... even the Promised Land is plagued by famine. Unfortunately, too many Christ followers don't really believe this. We tend to think that God blesses people by giving them pleasant circumstances. Sometimes, when adversity comes to those of us who believe, we get discouraged because we think God has abandoned us. We expect the faith we have in God to somehow exclude us from hard knocks. But that's not always how it works. You and I can be right where God wants us to be and still suffer setbacks and misfortune. That's how life works. Trials are the normal experience of God's people. Your life, especially if you are pursuing a life with God, will never be without the threat of trial and difficulty. God's will isn't always the easy and prosperous path. Often, it is gut wrenching.

Due to the famine, "Isaac went to Gerar, to Abimelech king of the Philistines" *(26:1b)*. In an attempt to preserve his wealth, in the form of many cattle, Isaac went to the land of the Philistines. While in Gerar or perhaps even before, Isaac decided to go down to Egypt just as his father had done. This seems like the logical thing to do since Egypt is where all the food is. Now Isaac isn't wrong for being concerned about the famine or feeding his family, but since we have no indication that God led this decision; he was wrong for failing to trust God to provide for his needs. And so, the Lord appeared to Isaac with this corrective word of instruction: "Do not go down to Egypt; stay in the land of which I shall tell you."

The first thing God does is **give Isaac a command**. He tells Isaac what not to do: **"Don't go down to Egypt! STAY PUT!"** This is the first time God appeared to Isaac.

Although Isaac is the miracle child of the promise given to his father Abraham, he is nonetheless facing famine, just as his daddy Abraham did in spite of receiving the promise *(Genesis 13)*. You might remember from your personal devotional reading that when Abraham faced a famine, he didn't consult the Lord; he just decided he had to "do something," so he packed up and moved to Egypt. He didn't renounce God's promise; he just forgot it under the pressure of circumstance.

When trouble strikes, we sometimes forget our knowledge of God, too. We struggle to recall past answers to prayer, specific guidance provided by the Holy Spirit, and lessons learned in previous crises. Only the present seems real. Our minds spin with future implications, and our troubled emotions inhibit clear thinking.

God tells Isaac, don't go down further south to Egypt. Gerar is still within the boundaries of the land God has promised to give to Abraham, Isaac, and their descendants. Egypt is not. So, God says, "Don't go there!" Listen. **It is better to experience famine and be**

where God wants you to be, than to run off to a place where you think life will be better but where God doesn't want you to be.

The Lord instructed Isaac to stay in the land of the Philistines for a while (enemy territory at that time), and the Lord said, "I will be with you and will bless you." Isaac's stay was to be "for a while." We can all identify with being in an uncomfortable place "for a while."

Are you in a bad situation right now? **God wants to provide for you in the midst of your impossible circumstances.** He wants you to trust him in the midst of your apprehension and uncertainty. The Word of God teaches us again and again that the safest place in the world is in God's will, for God will never lead us where his grace can't provide for us. It has been said, "Unbelief asks, '*How* can I get out of this?' while faith asks, '*What* can I get out of this?'" Today, in the midst of your painful and challenging predicament, will you ask God to grant you perseverance? He's big enough to handle your distress, and he will meet you right in the midst of it.

God tells Isaac, "I don't want you to go where you think you could get away from all the difficulty, I want to walk through this difficulty with you. Don't trust what you see, trust me, I have promised and I will not let you fail."

It's called the location principle: **God is very particular about the location.** During a famine you must be in the right place for God to provide and do his work. Location is the will of God for you. Don't, under pressure, move out from God's placement of your life. Isaac was not to change locations and go to Egypt.

Another lesson we learn from this narrative is that we have to be careful not to **repeat old patterns of failure.** It's a common pattern for children to repeat their parents' mistakes. Children of abusers have a stronger tendency to become abusers themselves. Children of alcohol and drug addicts have a stronger tendency to become addicts themselves. Children of greedy people or dishonest people tend to fall into the same traps that their parents did. That's just how it goes. It's sobering to realize that our sin doesn't just affect us; it affects others. If you are a parent, how you live serves better to teach your kids than almost anything else. Someone has said, "Young people never do an adequate job of obeying their elders, but they never fail to emulate them." That's the real issue here: imitation.

The Lord warns Isaac that he's facing the same things as his father and tells him, "Don't do what Daddy did." Isaac listens and does the right thing by not going to Egypt. He stays in Gerar. God wants us to stay where the promise is. It may look dry or unpromising, it may be surrounded by pressures, problems or poverty, but God wants us to neither move from where he has placed us; nor take things into our own hands.

It is the very nature of faith to hold on to what God promises even though the reality of those promises is not at the moment experienced. If every time we pray, our prayers got answered the way we wanted them to be answered, there would be little faith in our hearts. But if we become people who pray, and pray and pray, being certain of God's faithfulness even though all we experience is famine — that is faith.

Here's one more thought. **Face the famine by positioning yourself for blessing.** In Genesis 26:3, the Lord instructs Isaac, "Stay here in this land and I'll be with you and bless you. I'm giving you and your children all these lands, fulfilling the oath that I swore to your father Abraham. I'll make your descendants as many as the stars in the sky and give them all these lands. All the nations of the Earth will get a blessing for themselves through your descendants."

This section ends with a note of Isaac's obedience: "So Isaac lived in Gerar" *(26:6)*. After his visitation from God, Isaac responded with obedience. He obeyed God even though it didn't make much sense in the natural. He trusted that God would provide for him in the supernatural.

Your situation may appear impossible too, the very opposite of what God has promised. Be encouraged, the Lord is with you and present in the midst of the impossibilities you may be facing. The Lord is with you to give you strength and encouragement — because the Lord is with you, a better day will come! Amen and Hallelujah!

CHAPTER SEVEN

A Place Called Wits' End

"Why does God give light to man at his wit's end?" — Job 3:20, FT

[23]*Some went down to the sea in ships, doing business on the mighty waters;* [24] *they saw the deeds of the* LORD, *his wondrous works in the deep.* [25] *For he commanded and raised the stormy wind, which lifted up the waves of the sea.* [26] *They mounted up to heaven, they went down to the depths; their courage melted away in their calamity;* [27] *they reeled and staggered like drunkards and were at their wits' end.* [28] *Then they cried to the* LORD *in their trouble, and he brought them out from their distress.*

— Psalm 107:23-30, NRSV

The Book of Job is one long agonizing "why." Something has certainly gone wrong in the life of Job of Uz. Job was not only troubled by trouble, but Job was troubled by the extent of his trouble. He could understand some trouble, but the trouble in Job's life escalated. A mounting crescendo of trouble had overtaken him. Job saw his earthly possessions taken away. His oxen, his donkeys, his camels were all rustled off; his sheep were burned up; his servants were massacred; all of his children were killed when a cyclone struck his oldest son's house. Catastrophe, misery and misfortune descended upon this man so rapidly that he could scarcely get back on his feet before he was knocked down again. When failing health and disease overtook him, Job realized that he was at the end of his human wit. While he was cursing the day he was born, he whispered a sentence that deserves a place among the great sayings of all times: "Why does God give light to man at his wits' end?" These words give the name to the most tragic spot on any map, the place called wits' end.

Wits' end is a strange out-of-the-way place. It's one of life's inevitables. It's a place of exasperation and despair. It's the place where our weaknesses are on full display — a place where our limitations become transparent. To be at your wits' end is to have attempted and exhausted every possible means to solve a problem. Wits' end means we're out of options — we're out of ideas — we're out of patience, we don't know what to say or what to do. This phrase — wits' end — means, "To have come to the place where there is no perceived way out." It is the end of all human ability and resources. The word "trouble" in the Hebrew tongue means "to be restricted, to be tied up in a narrow, cramped place." And to be at your wits' end is to be in trouble.

Job wondered aloud, "Why does God give light to man at his wit's end?"

It's interesting to note that time and time again Jesus — the brightness of God's glory and the Father's comprehensibility and visibility — helped and made himself known to people at their wits' end. The lame, the blind, the crippled, the woman who was tormented twelve years with an issue of blood ... were all at the end of their wits.

Let me go deeper. When we are at our wit's end, we see it as a sign of weakness or failure — we see it as irrefutable evidence that our lives are spinning out of control. And in that situation, it's hard to see much hope. The scribbler of Psalm 107 describes how a group of sailors ran into a storm at sea. The clouds became gray with rain. Lightning danced its mysterious skeleton dance across the black bosom of the vaulted dome. The winds began to howl like angry wolves and the waves began to lap at the bow of the ship like 10,000 siccing dogs. The ship was tossed like a plaything and jostled about like browned leaves carried by a swift autumn breeze. And though the sailors were familiar with the twists and turns — the ebb and flow of the tides, all their strategies and skills were useless. Picture these scrambling men amidst the crashing waves, and the salty spray pounding the deck. These men have no hope; nowhere to go but down. The psalmist says, "They ... are at their wits' end."

The storm wasn't their doing. Nature has its own agenda. Sometimes we come to our wit's end due to circumstances beyond our control.

You've been there, too, haven't you? Trouble on top of trouble? Why did I lose my job at this time — with a thousand-dollar-amonth plus house note? Why are my children making failing grades in school while other folks' children are making the honor roll? Why is it that her house is happy and mine is a living hell? Why is it that I'm disturbed emotionally? Why can't my nerves settle down? Why is my body falling apart? Is God there? Is God available? Is God real? If relief exists, you can't think of it. The cancer hasn't gone away — your family or church is in shambles — your child hasn't come back home — your estranged spouse will stop at nothing but divorce, and you are desperate.

Truth is, more often than not we come to our wits' end because of our own indecision and bad choices. We seem to forget the boomerang principle — "What goes around, comes around."

Several years back an acquaintance of mine fell and broke his leg. When I saw him on crutches weeks later, I asked him what happened ... how did he break his leg? He replied, "Bell, it was my fault. I just didn't watch my step."

If only we would "watch our step." That's why we frequently find our loftiest hopes extinguished — our deepest affections abrogated — our noblest efforts checkmated — and our best laid plans disrupted — because we fail to watch our step!

Time after time we come to the end of our wits crying, "Now what can I do?" There is only one answer to the question: turn to God; for God gives us light at wits' end. The good news about being at our wit's end is that God meets us there.

It was at wits' end that Job found something better than human wit. He found God! These frantic sailors could do nothing to help themselves — the Hebrew poet says, "their wisdom was swallowed up." Everything they tried failed. It was only when the staggering sailors realized they were at the mercy of Almighty God and "they cried to the Lord in their trouble, and he delivered them from their distress" *(Psalm 107:28)*. It is only when they cried out to the Lord that they found deliverance. And then, of course, it was God's delight to calm the storm, to bring deliverance.

Mark this down: the Lord hears and answers the cries of desperate people — and I'm going to trust him because I know God is good.

El Shaddai is the Hebrew name for God that means God can take care of any situation. Just in case you might have COVID amnesia ... I have a question for you! Has God ever done anything for you at all? Has God ever healed you of a sickness? Has he ever delivered you from fear and defeat when you knew you were scared out of your wits and down for the count? If God has done it just for you then you owe God glory for all the great things he has done!

CHAPTER EIGHT

Overwhelmed

"From the end of the earth I will cry to you, when my heart is overwhelmed; lead me to the rock that is higher than I."
—Psalm 61:2, NKJV

Life has a way of bringing us to the point where we feel completely overwhelmed. So many of us are overwhelmed by things that keep us from living the life God wants for us. We struggle with things like insecurity, addictions, rejection, deadlines, bills, chronic health problems, family responsibilities, work-related drama ... your kids don't understand *or don't seem to care* that you're doing everything you can for them, *or* the unrealistic and stressful expectations of your relationships. Sometimes we feel overwhelmed by one big thing, other times we feel overwhelmed by many small things and, frankly, sometimes we feel overwhelmed by imagined circumstances or even the story we tell ourselves in our minds. Both men and women feel overwhelmed with all the chaos, clutter, and wreckage staring them in the face.

Overwhelmed! A feeling that the magnitude of the task at hand is too big to handle. **Overwhelmed!** Being put in the position of having to do things you've never done before. **Overwhelmed!** Being put in or caught up in circumstances where you don't know what to do. All of these feelings have one thing in common— **fear.** The core of being overwhelmed is **fear** —being afraid of the unknown and lacking confidence in our abilities to deal with the unexplored and unfamiliar.

When you're overwhelmed, it can be difficult to think and act rationally, and even function in a normal way. I can say with confidence that God doesn't want us to live lives characterized by stress and frustration.

Here are 3 common causes of feeling or being overwhelmed. Sometimes they can happen all at once!

1. **Fear of "bad" outcomes.** There are times when we really want something to go a particular way — and we can do everything we can to influence the outcome, but there may still be a lot of fear of the "bad" outcome happening. This fear can get intense and cause us to feel overwhelmed. Job said *(3:23)*, "What I always feared has happened to me. What I dreaded has come true."

2. **Uncertainty.** Uncertainty has a way of unnerving us almost to the point of paralysis. **What if the decision I've made is the wrong decision?** Uncertainty puts us in an extremely uncomfortable state and we cover our uncertainty with a pretense that says everything is well. We feel overloaded with life but somehow, we manage to keep up the front that seemingly says that all is well.

3. **Not having the answers to tough problems.** When we have a problem, we want an answer now. We want to fix it ASAP. But sometimes it's not that easy. When we're faced with a tricky problem and struggling to find a solution, we can find ourselves experiencing anxiety, worry and letdown. What we really need to do though is the opposite ... relax. Stressing when we need to come up with a creative solution to a challenging problem just makes things more difficult. Stress interferes with creative thinking.

If you feel overwhelmed — if you feel like you are so far behind that you can never catch up, this chapter is about some things you can do to get over being overwhelmed.

Right now, I lead or am part of the leadership of five separate groups or organizations. I'm pastor of a growing Church. I'm actively mentoring or coaching a half-dozen pastors and another half-dozen layfolk. And, not too long ago, I found myself moving in a dozen different directions. The most frustrating aspect of it all was that when I went to the office, I had no clear idea of what I should be doing. I didn't know where to start. I knew how I wanted things to be — I knew how they were supposed to be — but I couldn't figure out how to get from where I was (totally overwhelmed) to where I should be. The principles that I'm going to talk to you about today put me where I needed to be.

And this is the first thing I want you to remember? **Be in the moment.** If your thinking is focused on what the future holds — whether in a few minutes or several years down the road — it may make you more susceptible to becoming overwhelmed. Think about one assignment, task, and experience at a time, in the present moment, to help remove the possibility of uncontrollable thoughts that may or may not come about.

Be in the moment ... then, **define your priorities**. Understanding that your time and energy are not limitless means choosing how to use that time and energy. When you feel you have too much to do, start by identifying what matters most. At some point, in the midst of all our deadlines and commitments, we have to decide, as singer, songwriter and musician Bob Seger sang back in the day, "what to leave in and what to leave out." This requires that we take an inventory of our personal pantry — make a list of all of our obligations — and decide what needs to stay and what needs to go.

Too often we add things to our schedule, not because we believe it is what God wants us to do, but because we believe it will make us look good in the eyes of others. The Apostle Paul was aware of this tendency when he said to the Galatians, "Am I trying to win the approval of men, or of God? Or am I trying to please men? If I were still trying to please men, I would not be a servant of Christ" *(Galatians 1:10)*.

There is enough time in every day to do the things God wants you to do. If you are overwhelmed — if you have more to do than you can possibly get done — it is because you have added some things to the list that God didn't endorse. The only thing you can do at this point is axe everything that doesn't belong. This will subject you to criticism and will make some people unhappy, but the question is: are you trying to please God or impress people?

There is another thought I need to share with you ... **Take charge of the situation**. No matter what solutions you come up with to your dilemma, **it's now time to take full responsibility and start moving forward.** In other words, commit yourself to taking charge of the situation. Yes, there will be things and aspects that you still won't be able to control. However, **don't allow these things to distract you from everything else that you can do right now.** With this in mind, **focus on what can be controlled and work through these tasks one small step at a time.** Even if you can't do it all, you can at the very least begin somewhere. Start small and slowly build momentum one mini-task at a time.

Finally, **Trust God.** Now ... here's where it gets interesting. Stop judging God by what you are going through. Check out Hebrews 13.5-6. God said he will not leave us or forsake us. If he is a God that is true to his word, he meant what he said. You will go through things; you can't avoid the trials of life, but God will see you through them. God won't ever leave you. Isaiah 43:2 assures us that when we go through a trauma or a significant change God is with us. This is the "withness" of God.

Consider Paul's words in Romans 8:31: "If God is for us, who can be against us?" And Jesus reminds us that "with God all things are possible" *(Matthew 19:26)*. With God's help, we should be able to cast aside fear and anxiety. We should be able to focus on what is appropriate and possible—and then do it.

God is for us, not against us! If God were out to get us, we would be got by now! The moments when we feel like all we can do is pray are the moments when we recognize prayer is our greatest weapon *(Matthew 21:21-22)*. Prayer isn't one thing we can do, it's the best thing we can do.

Now, I have resolved to stop asking, "Why are you letting this happen to me, God?" Instead, my prayer is, "God show me what I need to learn and grow through this circumstance and help me trust that you have overcome." Amen and hallelujah!

CHAPTER NINE

Missing Spain But Getting A Dungeon

⁹For God, whom I serve with my spirit by announcing the gospel of his Son, is my witness that without ceasing I remember you always in my prayers, ¹⁰ asking that by God's will I may somehow at last succeed in coming to you. ¹¹ For I am longing to see you so that I may share with you some spiritual gift to strengthen you— ¹² or rather so that we may be mutually encouraged by each other's faith, both yours and mine. ¹³ I want you to know, brothers and sisters, that I have often intended to come to you (but thus far have been prevented), in order that I may reap some harvest among you as I have among the rest of the Gentiles.

— Romans 1:9-13, CEB

If there is one predictable thing in this life, it is that you will be disappointed somehow. Disappointment is common to everyone — and it often happens when we least expect it. You feel disappointed when something happens that defeats your hope for something you wanted. Someone once said, "Expectation is the root of all heartache." The quote recognizes that **when we experience disappointment, our hopes and expectations are out of line with reality**.

Paul — Chief among the Apostles ... God's most active ambassador ... and the Church's most celebrated preacher — traveled around the Greco-Roman world spreading the Good News. In this pericope, Paul talks to the Roman believers about how he has his heart set on taking the gospel to Spain. He had *charted* his course — he had *mapped* his travel itinerary to include a missionary journey to Spain. **But** he never got there. **He never gets to Spain** — and it's not his fault. He tries his best. But he fails in the end. He doesn't reach his goal. His mission of spreading the Good News to the ends of the earth is derailed. He is arrested and thrown into prison. All Paul wanted to do was to share in the joy of fellowship with the people of Spain, but, instead, he finds himself stuck in prison — with a dungeon cell as his forwarding address. His hopes were choked off — his dreams were crushed — his plans were frustrated, his aim and aspiration to preach the Good News of Jesus Christ had to be ditched ... put on the shelf of *things left undone*. **He wanted Spain — and got a dungeon cell.**

If we were to allow God to open the eye of our understanding we would see that Paul's experience of having his plans disrupted by life itself, has something to say to us. Somewhere along the road we have all dealt with disappointment — with postponed plans —

deferred hopes — and unrealized dreams. Every person's life is a diary in which he or she means to write one story and is forced to write another. **Paul wanted Spain — and got a dungeon cell.**

Disappointment. We want something to happen, and we believe/feel that it should happen due to our own needs, desires or situations and then — BAM — nothing. So, we get disappointed. What do you do when it happens to you? What do you do when the love of your life walks out and slams the door? What do you do when your dreams suddenly fall apart and you know there is no putting them *back* together again? How do we to go on when our world gets turned topsy-turvy ... when there is a fundamental breakdown in values ... when racism and intentional discrimination go mainstream? How can we make sense of our life when everything collapses? How many times have we planned for happiness and found sorrow couching and camping at our doorsteps? How often has the mountain of hope turned into a valley of weeping? We hoped for something big and it never happened. We fail exams we needed to pass to get into that elite college or university. Our dream job or career never materializes. How do we keep putting one foot in front of the other when nothing makes sense anymore? How do you not allow the disappointments in life to cause you to give up on life, give up on faith, and even give up your hopes?

Maybe you've wrestled with questions like these. Maybe you're even wrestling with them right now. Everyone has suffered from the distress of disappointment in one form or another. If so, I have a word of hope for you.

And this is the first thing I want you to remember: If you miss Spain and get a dungeon, however that may disappoint you, chose to **learn from it.** Instead of getting lost in the pain and negative emotions that can come from a disappointment, choose to see it more as something you can learn valuable things from *(and something that will help you to grow).*

Life is like the art of photography; we develop from our negatives. Life's disappointments may have a developing component to it if we allow the trials to have its perfect work. Some of the most poignant and priceless pictures comes, as you know, from negatives. The negatives of life do not have to make you the negative you experience, they can ultimately become the process that produces the picture that God desires.

"Whenever I take my journey to Spain ... " Paul never took that journey. Instead, he journeyed to Rome — and there he sits in a dungeon, scribbling on a bit of parchment. And, instead of feeling sorry for himself or falling out with God, Paul chose to learn from his disappointments and was better for them!

Now, let me download this second thought into the hard drive of your spirit: **When you miss Spain and, instead, get a dungeon cell, refocus on what you still have in your life. See, the key question is — how do you move away from disappointment?** To move on shift your focus to what you still have in your life. What does Paul do when he's tied down in a Roman prison? Well, he continues to do what he's been doing all along: he shares the good news to anyone who will listen — to prison guards, to friends who may come to visit, to strangers, to fellow prisoners, to anyone and everyone.

So often coming out of a crisis we underestimate what we still have left. You may have to start all over again. You may have to lose your home. You may have to let go of something or someone. But if you still have the presence of God, you are tremendously blessed! **God's presence in our present moments of crisis, uncertainty and disappointment invites us to cling to God's words in the fight of our lives.**

The hope of the Gospel is that God promises through Jesus Christ that we will never be abandoned. Life may be full of all kinds of hurts, disappointments, challenges, difficulties, and problems. But the trajectory of God's presence in our lives is fixed by the love of God. Regardless of our condition or circumstance, God is with us. There is never a moment in life when God has abandoned you.

Here is the shouting part for me. When Paul couldn't make it to Spain to enjoy the fellowship of a new community there, he finds the joy of God's presence in prison. Paul finds fellowship and communion in the least expected place. As Paul says elsewhere, "nothing shall separate him from the love of God."

I'm big on the presence of God because without the constant strength and comfort of God in Jesus Christ, we would be up the creek and doomed to failure; we would be without light, love, warmth, goodness, peace, life, all the things God is. Jesus embodies God with us. In our very midst, he is the revelation of God's character and passion.

Back in old Church, we used to sing hymns in worship. There was no praise team, just faithful congregants singing hymns. One song that seemed to almost always be on the musicians' playlist went like this:

> No! Never alone.
> No! Never alone.
> He promised never to leave me.
> Never to leave me alone!

Isn't that worth an "Amen?" God has promised never to leave us alone — never, no not ever, no never leave us behind, abandon us, or give up on us!

CHAPTER TEN

Making Hay While The Sun Shines

[5]After I have gone through Macedonia, I hope to see you [6]and visit with you for a while. I may even stay all winter, and then you can help me to continue my trip, wherever it is I shall go next. [7]I do not want to see you now while I am just passing through. Instead, I hope to stay a longer time with you if the Lord permits. [8]But I will stay at Ephesus until Pentecost, [9]for a wide door for effective work has opened to me, and there are many who oppose me.

— 1 Corinthians 16:5-9, CEV

Doors provide us privacy and security. They keep the cold air out of our homes in the winter and the cool air of our air conditioning in during the summer. And occasionally we use the term **door** in a figurative manner like when we speak of a "door of opportunity." This phrase "door of opportunity" speaks to our chance to do something new or different. Perhaps we have a door of opportunity to begin a new relationship *or* start a different job *or* purchase a new house *or* receive a fresh start *or* take a trip we've always wanted to take. But, I'm sure you already know, that like perishables ... opportunities expire. Every opportunity has a limited shelf life. A door of opportunity does not always stay open — and if we fail to walk through it *at the right time*, then we may never get the opportunity again.

Near the close of his First Corinthian correspondence, the Apostle Paul tells the believers at Corinth of his travel plans and how his intentions were to visit with them after spending some time traveling to and through Macedonia, the main province of northern Greece. Paul's plan was to spend the winter in Corinth ... if the Lord permits. This reflects how the Apostle was always subject to the will of God above his own.

Paul had built the church there in Corinth. And he wants to spend time with these folks. And so, he's planning things out — and he says, "I'm going to be there." And then he says in verse 7, "I hope to spend some quality time with y'all ... if the Lord permits."

Everything that Paul did was in pencil. He would plan, but he'd plan in pencil because it was "if the Lord permits." He was led by the Lord. And sometimes God didn't tell him, *as he was planning in pencil*, what was going to happen. Paul had to just go as the Lord led him here, led him there, he just flowed with it.

Doing the Lord's work means that you are viscerally and ultimately open to the Lord — you're led by the Lord — you're letting

God guide your steps. You're not saying, "Well, this is what I want to do." That's not the Lord's work; that's your work. So, you just have to say with Jesus, "Not my will, but your will be done." And sometimes you're going to want to go in a particular place and the Lord says, "No, I want you to go over here." So Paul wanted to spend the winter with them in Corinth, but he says, "Hey, all of this is in pencil because it has to do with the Lord. If the Lord permits."

In the meantime, Paul intended to prolong his stay in Ephesus — the place from where he is writing this letter to them — "until Pentecost" — because, he says, "a wide door for effective service has opened to me."

A "wide door" is used here metaphorically for opportunity. An open door is an opportunity that can lead us to a place where we can use our gifts, abilities, and talents to serve God and bless others. A "wide open door" is an invitation to pursue our own dreams and ideas — and no matter how tired, weak, or overwhelmed we are we must walk through them. A "wide open door" is an opportunity provided *by* God to act *with* God and *for* God. There was a big, wide-open door in Ephesus, and he says it was for "effective service." And God opened it up for Paul, and Paul spent three years there. Paul was taking full advantage of this open door. He was "making hay while the sun shines."

Paul said something in Ephesians 5:16 that we need to rehear today: "Make good use of every opportunity you have, because these are evil days."

Doesn't that really describe our world to a "T"? I can't say for sure that we're living in the "last days," but I can testify that we're living in "evil days." When a Black jogger named Ahmaud Arbery is murdered in February and an arrest is not made until May — these are evil days! When dollars mean more than lives — these are evil days!

"Make good use of every opportunity you have ... " **Pursue it when you see it!** Time is fleeting. You only get one opportunity to use the time you have today to the glory of God. You have heard all of the clichés ...

time waits for no one ...
opportunity knocks ...
seize the moment ...

But what Paul is talking about in this sentence to the Ephesian believers *and to us* is not a cliché; it is to be a way of life for those of us who are badge-wearing, card-carrying members of the household of faith! Paul encourages you and me — he bends our ears as believers in Christ — to make the most of our opportunities for the Lord, to seize the opportunity that the Lord gives to you and me, and in doing so we will give glory to God. We need to act when the opportunity presents itself because opportunities pass. When opportunity knocks open the door. When nobody is knocking build a door. When you see an opportunity, grab the moments, seize it like there is no tomorrow!

Too many of us miss out on great opportunities because we haven't made the necessary preparations to step through the door when it opens. We are the persons we are today because of the decisions we have made. However, what is equally true is that all of us are the persons we are today because of the decisions we have not made. Not to decide is to decide. If we don't decide, someone or something will decide for us. When we fail to decide, we miss opportunities and are faced with fewer options.

Don't miss your opportunities because you can't see pass your current situation or you are too busy chasing someone else's dreams. Don't let your opportunity pass because you are looking through the wrong door.

Even though Paul acknowledges in verse nine that a "a wide door for effective work has opened to me," it doesn't mean that everything was easy and went as expected, because he goes on to say in that same verse "**and there are many who oppose me.**" Now, with the open door, you have effective service. But you also have opposition. So, God's open doors are evidenced not only by effectiveness, but opposition. Just because God opens a door for us with many opportunities it does not mean it will always be easy.

One of the ways you can tell when the Lord is at work is the presence of opposition. If there is no opposition, then you've got to wonder, "Okay, am I in the right place? Am I doing the right thing? Am I really doing the work of the Lord, because we're getting no opposition from the enemy?"

Open doors are opportunities not guarantees. Going through an open door doesn't mean life will be easy. There is a natural tendency to think that when God opens doors, when "opportunity knocks," that everything will go smoothly, and you won't have any trouble, hardship, or failure. But the Word of God tells us that the opposite is true: that when God opens the door of opportunity so you can be used by him, it not only comes with blessing and fruitfulness, but many times it will come with paradox and opposition. But Paul wasn't intimidated or deterred by opposition. He believed that somehow, some way God is working in all things for good. Paul was confident that no matter what life throws at us, God knows what we need.

CHAPTER ELEVEN

Fight Instructions

[12] Don't join in the schemes of the people and don't fear what they fear. Don't take on their worries. [13]It is the LORD Almighty whom you should hold sacred, whom you should fear, and whom you should hold in awe.

— Isaiah 8:12-13, FT

The referee in boxing is the individual charged with enforcing the rules of that sport during a match. Once the boxers have been announced, the referee will greet them in the center of the ring and give them their pre-fight instructions: "I gave you your instructions in the dressing room. Remember protect yourself at all times and above all obey my command at all times. Let's have a clean fight, touch hands, back to your corners."

Too many Christians don't even realize we are living on a battlefield not a playground! Consider the words to the old hymn Onward Christian Soldiers. "Onward, Christian soldiers, marching as to war, with the cross of Jesus going on before. Christ, the royal Master, leads against the foe; forward into battle see his banners go!"

In Isaiah 8 we find our fight instructions. The prophet Isaiah had prophesied a great victory for the people of Judah, but when the Judeans found themselves surrounded by the armies of two small countries — Syria and Israel, they panicked and Ahaz, their king, sought help from another country. So, Ahaz forged an alliance with the even more formidable power of Assyria. The prophet Isaiah warned Judah's King Ahaz against aligning Judah with Assyria, but Ahaz was so afraid that he didn't think clearly. He was so afraid of the immediate threat of Syria and Israel that he failed to fear, as he needed to, the mightier power of Assyria. Ahaz and Judah made the mistake of appealing to Assyria for help. It was like asking a lion to rescue a flock of gazelle from two wild dogs. That of course stopped Syria and Israel from attacking Judah, but it also brought Judah itself under the domination of Assyria.

God even authorized Isaiah to give Ahaz a message, "Don't make a deal with the Assyrians. Don't fear what the people of Judah fear."

Everyone has fears and most everyone thinks that fear is a bad thing. But fear isn't entirely bad. Fear keeps you from sticking a fork into an electric socket. Fear keeps you from eating every berry you find on a hike. Fear keeps people from driving as fast as their car can go. Fear alerts you to danger.

But people often fear the wrong things. Fear is not a bad thing. But our fears are often misplaced. Someone once said that "Fear is the wrong use of imagination. It is anticipating the worst, not the best that can happen."

Misplaced fear is fear of the wrong thing. In other words, faith in the wrong thing produces the wrong fear. And faith in the wrong thing is at the root of so many of our problems, the worst of our miseries, and the heart of our sin: "For whatever does not proceed from faith [in God] is sin" *(Romans 14:23).*

All around us people fear the future; they worry about money; they fret about their health. They have great anxiety over world events, and yet the most often repeated directive in Scripture (114 times) is two simple words: "fear not." I hear people say, "I am afraid I am going to lose my job." "I am afraid that this marriage is not going to last." "I am afraid about the future of my children." "I am afraid of my results." What they do not realize is that they are surrounded by fear instead of faith and very soon it will be a reality. Job of Uz said in Job 3:25-26, "What I feared has come upon me; what I dreaded has happened to me. I have no peace, no quietness; I have no rest, but only turmoil." Job had a problem; when everything was going good, he was afraid and worried all the time. The result of Job's fear was that what he feared came upon him. Fear gives the enemy permission to attack us.

Listen. God can take us from fear to faith. It's been said, "If we're trusting the One who holds the last minute, we need not fear the next minute."

God, through Isaiah, warns us not to fear what the people fear; instead, honor the Lord and fear him. In fact, there is nothing else to fear. The life of those who are God's children is to honor the Lord and fear him alone. We have a clear choice: to fear God or to fear everything else; to trust God or to trust nothing.

Fear reveals what we trust. Our fears show how we're relying on our own efforts and not trusting in the God of Jesus Christ. Craig Groeschel, the founder and senior pastor of the multi-site Life.Church is credited with saying, "What we fear the most often reveals where we trust God the least." The things that often keep us awake at night, relentlessly pacing the floor, are the things that we aren't trusting God to handle. So, we place our trust in government and gunpowder, money and the acquisition of things, and the list goes on and on.

Fear creates forgetfulness of God's promises. When a Christian is fearful, it is a sign that he or she has forgotten the promises of God. It is especially important for God's people to memorize scripture passages that contain promises of God's presence, love and power in our lives. Studying the lives of Bible figures can help as well. We learn that many of them went through extremely dangerous and difficult circumstances but came out victorious because God was with them, and he kept his promises.

Fear generates unfaithfulness toward God's purposes. When we fear, we are unlikely to obey God. Yet, when we trust God, we will do anything God asks of us. Fear keeps many people from serving God faithfully. I have known people with great gifts who refused to serve because of fear. Yet, I have known others who were mediocre in terms of their talents, but they served and were greatly used of God because they had a deep faith that overcame their fears.

"Don't fear what they fear. Don't take on their worries." Change your focus. Put your focus on God. Take your eyes off the problem and yourself and look at Jesus. The poet of Psalm 56:3 testifies, "When I am afraid, I put my trust in you."

As long as I focus on the fear, it is not going to get smaller. The longer I focus on it, the bigger part of my life it consumes. The more it influences me. So, I change my focus.

Fear of the Lord can produce awe. The fear of the Lord is better described than defined. It is better experienced than analyzed.

Fearing the Lord means to be in awe of his holiness, to give the Lord his due reverence. This is not a fear that we *grow out of,* as if religion has somehow evolved away from it. This is a fear we *grow into*. We are to fear God as we love him, and we are to love him as we fear him. Both the Old Testament and the New Testament make this plain.

Remember, God has not given us the spirit of fear but a spirit of love and freedom to serve God faithfully. The Apostle Paul knew the secret to vanquishing fear and he expressed that secret in these words: "Nothing in all creation will be able to separate us from the love of God that is in Christ Jesus our Lord" *(Romans. 8:39)*. If you know that deep in your spirit, your faith will overcome any fear! Amen and hallelujah!

CHAPTER TWELVE

Fighting Back Against Falling Back

Demas has abandoned me. He fell in love with this present world and has gone to the city of Thessalonica.
— 2 Timothy 4:10, FT

One of the most frustrating, disconcerting, indeed discouraging facts every pastor has to face is the problem of people who have great potential and a great future for the kingdom, but somewhere along the way they take a wrong turn, and all that's left is "what might have been."

Demas is mentioned three times in the New Testament. In fact, in Philemon 1, verse 24, Paul refers to him as a "fellow worker." The word literally means "A companion in the work." Demas was one of the Apostle Paul's travelling companions. There was a time when Paul and Demas were laborers together with God. Then, in Colossians 4:14, Demas is mentioned to be working alongside of Luke.

But later on, in 2 Timothy, Paul says, "Demas has abandoned me" *(4:10)*. Demas is a perfect example of a man who started well and finished poorly. Demas travelled with Paul, ate with Paul, suffered persecution with Paul, and yet, somehow, somewhere along the line, something went wrong. Demas did a 180. He turned back. Demas had "starting power" but no "staying power."

Now the fact that Paul says "Demas has abandoned me," tells me not only of a present failure, but also of a past faithfulness. From the scriptures, we know that Demas was once a strong member of the Lord's Church. There was a time when Demas was sold out to God, but soon he faded and backslid.

Backsliding is not merely a problem for Biblical characters; it is an issue for the 21st Century Church. We all know the temptation to quit. One writer concluded, "The most important thing in life is not to run away." Do you feel the impact of that? And I'm not just talking about quitting in the little, insignificant, inconsequential things we become involved in. Often, we feel like quitting the significant things as well.

As I look back over my life, one of my regrets is about the good things I started but didn't finish. Have you ever been in that kind of place? I have. When I desperately wanted to throw in the towel, to throw up my hands. Can you think of things — good things — that you started and then quit? Perhaps you quit school. Perhaps you quit working on a troubled relationship. Maybe you quit at work. Or maybe there is something God called you to do — you gave it a try — and then you quit. Maybe you have quit in your Christian commitment. Oh ... you're still a member of the church, your name is still there. But your heart isn't. It's not a high priority. The fire has gone out. And, if you were honest, you would say that, by and large, you've quit.

Yes, the temptation to give up, to lose hope, to despair, is universal. It's not difficult to start, is it? We've started good things over and over again. But then the hours get long. The going gets tough. Some new interest strikes our fancy. And suddenly, the thing we started so enthusiastically has been abandoned.

Jesus said in Matthew 10:38, "You must take up your cross and follow me and anyone looking back is not worthy of me." How easy it is to start turning back to our old ways of living. The allure of the ordinary, the temptations of the flesh, and the weariness of the work can often cause people to turn back. It doesn't happen in an instant, but bit by bit, people find disappointment and then attractions elsewhere cause them to turn.

Please don't think that Demas' transition from "fellow worker" to "spiritual deserter" happened all at once. Demas was a fine follower of Christ for years. Demas became a backslider. *(A backslider is a Christian who has gone backward spiritually instead of forward.)* Backsliding is a very prevalent, present-day menace to Christianity! Proverbs 14:14 posits "The backslider in heart will be filled with his own ways." Backsliding seldom, if ever, happens in a moment, in the twinkling of an eye. Backsliding is not an EVENT, it is a gradual PROCESS. It doesn't occur overnight; it occurs over a period of weeks and months and even years. Backsliding is NOT like jumping off a cliff, but rather it's like slowly drifting down a long hill. It always results from a process. You see, Demas didn't wake up one morning out-of-the-blue and say, "I am through with the ministry. I've had it with the work of God. I'm tired of this kind of life. I want to eat, drink, and be merry and grab all the gusto that I can."

What motivated Demas to fall back, to abandon the fight? While Paul doesn't give us a specific answer, he does tell us the underlying problem. It is one that should challenge each of us deeply. Paul says, "Demas has abandoned me. He fell in love with this present world." Now the word "world" here does not refer to the material creation. We ought to love the physical world. God created this world and said it was good. There is a theology of ecology, and we are to enjoy what God has created. World in the context of this pericope refers to the "world system" ... where the ethics of convenience holds sway — where there are no fixed ethical imperatives — where there is a cognitive blackout of eternal truth.

The problem Demas had was that he turned his love from God to the world. We would call this a **misplaced love.**

Demas "loved this present world," and the word "loved" is derived from *agape*, the kind of all-consuming love that was exemplified by the life and death of Jesus, and which we are supposed to give to God first, and to others through the power God gives. Demas stopped *agape*-loving Jesus and started *agape*-loving this present world instead.

And once he made this choice, what did he do? Did he stick around, and give Paul a chance to talk him out of it? No. He went back to the place he got saved out of. He went home, as backsliders often do, far away from Paul. Paul said, "He has departed for Thessalonica," never to be heard from again. You see, one of the greatest tragedy of the backslider is that she or he loses her or his witness. The salt loses its savor.

How do we get back to God? Whatever you have to do each day, **fall in love with Jesus all over again.** Way back in the last century, there was a song with the lyrics, "Take me back ... Take me back, dear Lord ... To the place where I first received you. Take me back ... Take me back, dear Lord ... Where I first believed."

Finally, **get involved in the Lord's work.** Jesus said, in John 5:17, "My Father never stops working, and I work." Broadly speaking, the work of the Lord is anything to which we might lay our hands as Christians — both within the body of Christ and in seeking to minister to those outside the body of Christ. It is, as Paul notes in Colossians 3, that whatever we do, in word or in deed, we should do it all to the glory of the Lord Jesus. God created you and me to make a redemptive difference. We believe, ofttimes against the witness of a harsh reality, that one day justice will roll down like waters, and we work today for that justice, even if doing so means that we will be maligned and misunderstood. Our purpose is not to idly sit and observe life. We are commissioned and capacitated to respond the way Jesus did with the right use of all God has given us. And we are called to do our best.

CHAPTER THIRTEEN

Interrupted

[1]He left that place and came to his hometown, and his disciples followed him. [2]On the Sabbath he began to teach in the synagogue, and many who heard him were astounded. They said, "Where did this man get all this? What is this wisdom that has been given to him? What deeds of power are being done by his hands! [3]Is not this the carpenter, the son of Mary and brother of James and Joses and Judas and Simon, and are not his sisters here with us?" And they took offense at him. [4]Then Jesus said to them, "Prophets are not without honor, except in their hometown, and among their own kin, and in their own house."

— Mark 6:1-4, NRSV

Have you ever made plans to do something only to have those plans come to a screeching halt? You think you're going to accomplish a desired task *or* complete an assignment and then something happens, totally taking you in a different direction. Truth is that **life is filled with interruptions.** We've all made plans, haven't we? Maybe it was for an hour, a day, a weekend, or a vacation, our work, our finances, our family. And we've all experienced the interruption of those plans by circumstances that changed or the unexpected that happened. What is that they say about "The best-laid plans of mice and men often go awry ...?"

Life's interruptions are those times in life when things just don't seem to go the way we had planned. Interruptions can either make us or break us. We can learn from life's experiences, or we can become resentful and close ourselves off to all that God has for us.

Interruptions — a telephone call when we're rushing out the door for an important engagement — the guests who drop by uninvited — the loss of electric power when we're trying to finish an important email — having to leave work to pick up a child at school because of a stomach ache — severe financial reversal — loss of employment — divorce — a serious accident — an untimely death — a transfer in our job that takes us to an unfamiliar city ... and we could go on and on. Interruption is one of the most troublesome flies in the ointment of life. These interruptions don't announce themselves. Their seriousness is contingent on the nature of the interruption, but also on what's going on in our lives when they pop up. This COVID-19 pandemic is more than a snowstorm that slows things down for a few days, or a rainy day that forces us to cancel our plans. This is an interruption to many day-to-day routines for weeks and months to come.

Interruptions — they are as common as corn flakes. If we don't learn to cope with them, they will keep our nerves frayed — drain us of the energy we need to invest more meaningfully — drive us to distraction and play havoc with our relationships. How can we cope? The interruptions aren't going to go away; they'll keep popping up to invade our lives just when we're safest — life is just that way.

Jesus was often interrupted in his ministry ... and when he was, he didn't respond in anger, he didn't throw a temper tantrum and rant about how no one seems to respect his time. Let's look at how Jesus handled interruptions and learn from him.

Mark 6 follows an intense period of ministry in Jesus' life. Had we gone back to Chapter 5, we would have read the story of the deranged man who lived in a graveyard, whom Jesus ministered to, leaving him "clothed and in his right mind." We would have read of that ruler of the synagogue, Jairus, coming to Jesus, falling at Jesus' feet and begging him to come and heal his daughter who was at the point of death — and Jesus responded. We would have read that marvelous story of faith; a woman who had had a flow of blood for twelve years, pressing through the multitude and touching just the hem of his garment, and Jesus feeling that touch and responding to that woman's faith, saying, "Daughter, your faith has made you well; go in peace and be healed of your disease."

Following that period of intense ministry, and his sending his own disciples out to minister, Jesus realized that all of them needed rest and renewal. So, he suggested that they cross the Sea of Galilee and find an isolated place where they could get away from the crowds, pray together, rest, refocus and reset themselves on the work that lies before them. But as they make their way to that place of retreat, a throng of people found out where Jesus is going and interrupt him.

So, we need to look at Jesus, and learn from him, in order that our interruptions will not play havoc in our lives, but that we will be able to integrate those interruptions meaningfully.

First of all, **Jesus could integrate the interruptions into his life because he had a clear purpose.** That's the first word. Purpose.

Purpose is much less about the "what" and much more about the "why." Even the most annoying, insignificant "whats" can be done with a sense of joy and satisfaction if a person has the right "why." Purpose comes from knowing the "why" of our lives. "Why am I here?" "Why am I doing this?"

A life purpose is like a compass, guiding you over life's path, keeping you centered, focused and clear on what really matters to you and what you want from life. When you know the purpose of your life, you tend to live a more meaningful existence than those who don't. You tend to live each day to the fullest, because you know who you are, whose you are, where you're coming from, and where you're going.

To cope with interruptions, you must have purpose in life and keep that purpose distinct. Interruptions will not devastate us if we are clear about our purpose. The power of purpose was so evident in Jesus. He never lost sight of his purpose. He stated his purpose with crystal-clear clarity: "The Son of Man came not to be ministered unto but to minister" *(Mark 10:45)*.

Furthermore, we can cope with life's interruptions if we **keep the perspective that persons, not things, are of ultimate value**. When we have that perspective, we realize that life's love is interruptible. There's a word in our text — "As he went ashore, he saw a great crowd; and he had compassion for them, because they were like sheep without a shepherd."

When our life plans are interrupted it's easy and tempting to blame others — to go ballistic about why things aren't working out or pray that God will make it all go the way we want. But Jesus doesn't do any of that. Imagine Jesus as he nears the shore and catches a glimpse of thousands of people waiting to meet him. Most of us would be frustrated at the sight. We'd probably decide it best to send away the crowds. Or maybe we'd stay in the boat and go somewhere else. But that's not Jesus' response. He's not frustrated. He doesn't turn the boat around when he sees the crowd. He doesn't get angry or resentful. He doesn't blame or complain. He doesn't ignore or deny the interruption. Jesus was always able to stop for the needs of others. He has "compassion" on the crowd, and starts to teach them — and, eventually, feeds them.

Interruptions can be appointments for compassion. Life may feel unfair, but in your everyday routine recognize the Lord in the little things and love like Jesus. Loving people is the business of Jesus' followers — and ofttimes interruptions represent people to love and are opportunities for you to be loved!

There is one more thing to be said. **Interruptions require that you live by faith.** You respond by living by faith every day, instead of waiting on something to happen to search for God. When a major catastrophic event occurs, emotions are high and needs are great. If you are already living by faith, you can quickly call upon God for help. You gain comfort. You shun fear. You trust God for your safety. You are also positioned to encourage others who need help connecting with God's love, strength and guidance.

When you are confronted with life's interruptions, stay in faith and declare, "My situation may be impossible with man, but it is possible with God" *(Luke 18:27)*. Then allow God to turn that impossible situation in your life to your good and to his glory!

CHAPTER FOURTEEN

When Things Get So Bad You Want To Clock Out

[7] O LORD, you have enticed me, and I was enticed; you have overpowered me, and you have prevailed. I have become a laughingstock all day long; everyone mocks me. [8] For whenever I speak, I must cry out, I must shout, "Violence and destruction!" For the word of the LORD has become for me a reproach and derision all day long. [9] If I say, "I will not mention him, or speak any more in his name," then within me there is something like a burning fire shut up in my bones; I am weary with holding it in, and I cannot.

— Jeremiah 20:7-9, NRSV

Jeremiah is the author of the books Jeremiah and Lamentations. And it is no secret that he is referred to as the "weeping prophet."

Jeremiah was called at an early age to be a prophet to Judah. God tells young Jeremiah, in Jeremiah chapter 1, verse 5, "I chose you before I formed you in the womb; I set you apart before you were born." God knew Jeremiah — chose Jeremiah — and appointed Jeremiah. He was known by name, hand-picked by God, and commissioned to serve.

Like Jeremiah, before we were even conceived, God had a plan for our lives. When God created you — he gave you certain gifts, talents, and natural abilities to accomplish something he wanted you to do. We call that an assignment. And God already knew what we would need to carry out our assignment.

Don't miss this. Everything God creates is a solution to something. You are a life jacket to someone drowning. First of all, you are **geographically designed**. This means that your nationality, your race, sex, and even where you were born were decided by God.

You are **geographically designed** — and, secondly, you are **geographically assigned**. God does extraordinary things through ordinary lives and one of the ways this happens is that God gives us assignments. This means there is a place, a city, a location where God wants you.

You are **specifically assigned**. We all have a **specific assignment** from God. There is something that God has ordained for our lives. You are not wired to be a genius at everything, **BUT** you are wired to do some things well. God has an assignment for you that he has purposed for you to follow through on. When you step into your assignment *(big or small)* by faith, that's when you will find the "courage of your calling" as a Christ follower.

Jeremiah means **Jehovah appoints**. And wherever God **appoints**, he **anoints**. 1 John 2:27 says, "But the anointing that you received from him abides in you…" The anointing of God is the presence and power of the Holy Spirit operating through you to accomplish whatever God will be asking you to do for him.

And, wherever God **appoints**, he **anoints**. All of us have cried over what we have gone through while trying to do God's will. No matter what others tell us, we are **anointed for the assignment**. It is a test of our character. **God wants to know if you will represent him while you are going through what you are going through.** Anyone can shout when there is a mall in their closet or a traffic jam in the driveway *(from all the cars you own)*, but can you say "this is the day the Lord has made, let us rejoice and be glad in it" *(Psalm 118:24)* when it seems as if Murphy's Law *(Anything that can go wrong — will go wrong!)* is in full effect? It's about how you will act under pressure. So many of us are going through so much that we think the devil has nobody's address but ours. If you would look back over your life, you will realize that you should be dead or out of your mind by now, but you are still here because of your anointing. **You were anointed for your assignment.**

So then, Jeremiah was called to a great assignment, but Jeremiah felt that his assignment was too excessive for him. Jeremiah was ready to get out of the "prophecy business" altogether. The persecution that he endured as a result of doing what God called him to do compelled him to throw his hands up and tell the Lord that he wanted to quit!

What was the use of continuing to prophesy to an indifferent people? Why struggle against the inevitable? Why try to convince people who don't want to be convinced? Why not get away from it all and take it easy? I'm sure Harriet Tubman — believed to have helped some 300 slaves to escape — felt like Jeremiah at some time or another. Dr. Martin Luther King, Jr. was 29 years old and emerging as the leader of the civil rights movement when he was stabbed in the chest with a razor-sharp seven-inch letter opener by a deranged African American woman — and I'm sure there were times when he thought "I need to just preach at Ebenezer."

You were anointed for your assignment, and not only do you have an assignment from God, but the devil has an assignment against you. You see, the fulfillment of your God-given, God-sized assignment scares the devil the most. Nothing gives him as much pleasure as keeping you distracted. There are three things Satan loves to do to your assignment: (a) substitute it, (b) delay it, or (c) waste it. Most people die unfulfilled. The devil's favorite pastime is to substitute people's dreams.

How many times have you woke up on Sunday morning and looked in your closet and looked at your bed and decided you really didn't want to get up, get ready, get dressed come to the church house? How many times have you woke up in the middle of the night and looked at your spouse or thought about how much grief your child is giving you because she or he thinks she or he knows more than you or any other adult — and at least thought, even for a fleeting moment, that you should just leave?

Look at verse 7. Jeremiah felt deceived by God. Jeremiah expected that God was going to change things through his ministry — but nothing has happened. He felt that God had lured him into the ministry only to make him a laughingstock. He felt ridiculed and offended. His voice was not making a difference. He was crying out for the people to repent — and they ignored his every word — and continued toward destruction and judgment.

Listen. God wants us to talk to him, even when we are angry, upset, and frustrated. He wants us to tell the truth. A lot of dishonesty goes on in relationships, even with God. People often ask me: "Is it wrong to be angry with God?" And, then they're sometimes surprised by the answer I give them: "If you feel anger toward God you should tell him. God is big enough and strong enough to handle your hurt and anger. So, tell him about. He wants you to pour out your heart to him. He wants you to express what is in your heart."

John Ortberg, former Pastor of San Francisco's Menlo Park Presbyterian Church, once asked us this question: **"When did God ever give anyone an easy assignment?"** Think about every Bible story you've ever heard or read. They're all so remarkable and relevant because people like us were given incredibly difficult assignments and rose to the occasion. Moses was asked to lead a nation of slaves out of Egyptian bondage. Jonah was told to preach repentance to his enemies, the Ninevites. Gideon had to battle an army of Philistines with only 300 soldiers. David faced Goliath. Noah built a boat to survive a flood even though no one had ever even seen rain before. And then there was Jesus.

The thing is, when God gives us difficult assignments, they will always be too big to be humanly possible. Inherent in a God-sized calling is the need for uncommon faith. Why? **Because what God calls us to do will always be too big and too impossible to accomplish without God's help.**

Verse 9 is such a powerful statement. In verse 9 Jeremiah says that he wasn't even going to mention God's name anymore. Jeremiah was convinced that he was going to give up and let God get somebody else to do what he wanted him to do. So, he decides to stop. He's going to give up his ministry, and go back to farming, or whatever.

Many of us have the same testimony. I guarantee you that everyone who's in any kind of Christian ministry has had times when they've felt like this. Many years back, I pastored a small East Texas congregation. Within the first eighteen months, the church experienced exceptional growth, we remodeled the facility and giving increased by almost 1000 percent. But, the push back I received from traditionalists prompted me to have a Jeremiah moment.

Jeremiah said that the pressure is too great. But just when he thought life was over and he saw no hope, something sprung up within him. Jeremiah said "But, his word was in mine heart like a burning fire shut up in my bones." Jeremiah realized he could not stay in this rut another day.

Jeremiah's despair turned to joy — his defeated attitude turned to triumph — his dismay turned to courage. Jeremiah realized that he wasn't alone. He says in chapter 20, verse 11, "But the LORD is with me like a violent warrior." Jeremiah realized that he was not on the losing side. He was going to win because the Lord was with him like a mighty warrior. God would deal effectively, in his own way and time, with his enemies. It's that realization that emboldens us. Hallelujah and amen!

CHAPTER FIFTEEN

Shattered Dreams

"Don't call me Naomi," she responded. "Instead, call me Mara, for the Almighty has made life very bitter for me."

—Ruth 1:20, NLT

We all have dreams. I know you have dreams as well. Dreams for you, your family, your future, your right now, your life. Dreams how everything in the end turns out with a "happily ever after." But every once in a while, I have to reset. I have to struggle to regain my balance because my experience doesn't match my expectations. I have to take a strategic pause because my dreams have been shattered. And I know I'm not alone in this. Whether you're a kid, or an adult, or in mid-life, everybody experiences shattered dreams. And they can revolve around your career, your relationships; they can revolve around the kind of pain and dysfunctions that grow out of them.

There's a sister in Scripture named Naomi who experienced firsthand the struggle with shattered dreams. Naomi's story is found in the Book of Ruth.

The Book of Ruth is an interesting portrayal of three women — Naomi, Orpah, and Ruth. The story takes place during the time of the judges in Israel. According to the last verse of the book of Judges, it was a time of ineffectual political leadership: "All the people did what was right in their own eyes" *(Judges 21:25)*.

Not only was there **political instability**, but there was **economic disaster** as well — "there was famine in the land." Famine in the ancient Mediterranean meant bloated bellies of little children — older people dying in the streets — people wandering aimlessly begging for food. Against this brutal setting, Elimelech, his wife Naomi and their two sons flee from Judah, pack up all of their earthly possessions and head for the country of Moab, because he'd heard that things were better there. After their arrival in Moab, Elimelech dies leaving his wife Naomi alone with her two sons Mahlon and Chilion. The two sons marry Moabite women, Orpah and Ruth. Ten years later the husbands of Ruth and Orpah die leaving all three women widowed.

Naomi escaped the famine, but she ran into three funerals, and her dreams are shattered. She lost her husband. She lost her two boys. And she hears through the grapevine the news that the famine in Judah was over. And so, she decided it was time to go back home — and her two daughters-in-law travel with her. So, they apparently went far enough that Naomi thought it time to stop and send the girls back to Moab where they might stand a chance of "starting a new life."

Orpah "agreed" and kissed Naomi good-bye and headed back to Moab. However, Ruth emphatically said that she would go with Naomi to Judah and would stay there with her. Her statement of love and commitment is beautiful. It has on occasion served as a Scripture reading for weddings: "Where you go, I will go. Where you stay, I will stay. Your people will be my people, and your God my God. Where you die, I will die and there I will be buried" *(Ruth 1:16)*. But these were the words of a daughter-in-law to her mother-in-law!

Although her name means "sweetness" or "pleasant," after the death of her husband and sons Naomi has a bone to pick with God for the emptiness she feels. She's devastated. She's depleted. And not only has she lost so much, but she also believes it has happened because the Lord God Almighty is against her *(Ruth 1:13, 20)*. In her grief, she suggests that possibly God is responsible for their deaths. Naomi feels that she left Judah with a husband, two sons, and a promising future, and because of the Lord's doing she is returning empty-handed. She looks at the people and says, "Don't call me Naomi! Don't call me Sweetness! Stop calling me Pleasant. I'm dying inside. I have nothing. From now on call me Mara. Call me Bitter!"

Have you ever felt like Naomi? There is enough tragedy in the world, and enough unpleasantness at home that each of us could easily say, "call me Mara." Some of you are doing everything in your power to just keep it together long enough to get through the next few minutes. Some of the pain you carry is years old. The pain is real. It's as real as Naomi's.

I believe that it's okay for Naomi to be bitter and angry ... after all she has lost her husband and sons. Who wouldn't feel rained on? Anyone who has experienced what Naomi experienced will confess that their first response was one of bitterness and anger. Not only is it logical and understandable, but healthy. It is part of both the grieving and the healing processes. And please note that God doesn't condemn anyone for expressing anguish and indignation in the face of tragedy.

I think we'd all agree that Naomi was looking at shattered dreams. What's the truth about shattered dreams?

Well, for one thing, **we must face them.** No matter how painful… until you face the pain and the hurt, and the loss, and the disappointment, and the anger, and the frustration, and the resentment, you'll never grow. Most of us hide, compartmentalize, compensate, lash out, blame, internalize, and never grow through our shattered dreams.

You know why most people don't change? Really, it takes courage to change, to make a fresh start. You never can move from where you are, until you have the courage to face your dilemma, "This is where I really am. I have a problem. I'm disappointed. I have anger issues. I have an addiction. I'm in denial. Part of that marriage issue was my problem. My kids probably don't call me, one, because they're insensitive and this and that but they probably don't call me because I complain too much. I need to own this part of it."

And it's that facing of your shattered dreams that's painful. But now you know where you're at. Now you're ready to be a recipient of grace. I mean, sometimes we have to cry out for help, saying, "God, I need Your help."

So, face your shattered dreams. Painful, but God…what did we learn? The poet of Psalm 34:17 posits, "The Lord is near to the brokenhearted. He saves those who are crushed in spirit."

My point is simply this: **Life is a continual story of shattered dreams.** In an imperfect world, with imperfect people, you are going to have shattered dreams. Did you ever think of that?

No, it doesn't mean your dreams were wrong, it doesn't mean they're bad, but it means that in a fallen world God can use your shattered dreams, and my shattered dreams, to grow and prosper us even in loss. God can take that which is broken and put it together again and make it better than it was before. God can take the shattered pieces of our lives and make them strong in the places where they were once weak.

CHAPTER SIXTEEN

Limiting God

A man of God approached and said to the king of Israel, "Thus says the LORD: Because the Arameans have said, 'The LORD is a god of the hills but he is not a god of the valleys,' therefore I will give all this great multitude into your hand, and you shall know that I am the LORD."

— 1 Kings 20:28, NRSV

In 1 Kings 20, we find the Syrians were at war with Israel. In the previous year Israel had thoroughly defeated the Syrians in battle and Syrian King Ben Hadad had barely escaped the battlefield with his life.

Then, King Ben Hadad's National Security Council advisers had a brain-storming session in their effort to figure out why Israel had beaten them so convincingly before. Why did the Israelites love to fight in the hill country? Why were Israel's sacred shrines situated on hilltops? The Syrians had no doubt heard the Jews sing

Psalm 15 — "O LORD, who may abide in your tabernacle? Who may dwell on your holy hill?" Suddenly, a lightbulb went off in the minds of the King's advisers that in some way this Hebrew God was associated with the hills and mountains. So, they made what they considered to be logical conclusion based on deductive reasoning. They decided on changing their combat strategy. They said that they had fought on the hills and lost because Israel's God is a god of the hills *but* he is not a god of the valleys. They suggested to King Ben Hadad that "if we take the battle to the valleys we will surely be victorious." And, when they were ready to attack God's people using their new strategy, God had a surprise in store for them — and even in the valley the Syrians were defeated.

The Syrians made a serious miscalculation. They made a costly mistake. Their calculus was off. They had the cooked-up idea that God was "territorial" — that God was restricted — that God was limited in God's ability to deliver his people. And their error was due to the fact that they underestimated God. And, they are not alone in this misestimation. Oftentimes we, too, are guilty of the same fallacy. So this passage has something to teach us about God — and that is with God, when you least expect it — expect it.

And, this is the first thing I want to share with you. The Syrians said, "The LORD is a god of the hills but he is not a god of the valleys." The Syrians were half-blind to where God is. They saw God on the wild storm-swept hills, but not in the fertile valleys. And, isn't it true that in our assessment of the topography of our lives **we are often blind to just where God is.**

In Matthew 25, in his parable of the final judgment when the sheep will be separated from the goats — when the faithful and the unfaithful will be separated, one group is told that they have cared for Christ when he was hungry, thirsty, lonely, and naked; they had taken care of Christ when he was sick and when he was in prison. By contrast, the other group hadn't done any of these things for Christ. Notice that both groups of people ask the same question, "When was it that we saw you?" Neither the faithful or the unfaithful noticed God in their midst.

It is as if Jesus is telling us that **God regularly, even relentlessly, shows up just where we least expect God to be.** God showed up ... not in Jerusalem or Rome, but in a manger, a place for feeding cattle, in backwater Bethlehem in the vulnerable flesh of a baby. God showed up ... not in pomp and circumstance but in a brutal crucifixion on a skull-shaped hill outside the city walls of Jerusalem. Again and again, God in Jesus shows up where we least expect God to be to surprise us — disarm us — strengthen us — overturn our expectations and judgments, all in order to invite us to give up our attempts to go it alone and instead accept God's redemptive, surprising, and incomparable love.

The Syrians thought that God was only a God of the hills but not of the valleys.

Figuratively speaking, the hills represent the high points in our lives — the mountain-peak experiences — the times when we feel like we're on top of the world. And we know what the valleys represent ... don't we? The valleys represent the low times — the difficult times — the challenging times. Hills refer to our good times — and valleys refer to our bad times.

Some people have this idea that God is the God of our good times, but he is not there when we are going through arduous times. They think that God leaves us helpless in the valleys, especially when the troubles we experience are of our own making.

One thing is for certain ... life is not always lived on top of the hill where we feel safe and secure from all that looms on the horizon. Today, more than ever, we hear the desperate cries from the hurting edges of our day: "Where in the world is God?" Daily we witness so much that seems to contradict any faith and hope grounded in God's caring love. The absurdities of our contemporary culture are so noisy and threatening that they leave us numb, jittery and glassy-eyed. Rampant starvation, poverty, disease, and suffering leave millions in despair and pain daily. The cruel and brutish destruction of Black lives by those who have sworn to protect-and-serve. Personal tragedies multiply and evil flourishes. Others plead: "If there is a God, where is he when we need him the most?"

The penman of the Pentateuch recounts how Jacob, the favored son of Isaac, the son of Abraham, who had tricked his brother Esau out of his birthright and now Esau was so angry that he wanted to kill Jacob. One day Jacob was dreaming about a ladder that was set on the earth and rising all the way up to heaven. And angels are going up and down that ladder, getting closer to God and farther away from earth. And the voice of God called out to a surprised

Jacob and tells Jacob, "I'm with you and I'll take care of you wherever you go and bring you back here…and I will not leave you" *(Genesis 26:15)*. And in that valley moment Jacob shouted, "Surely God is in this place…and I didn't know it" *(Genesis 28:16)*.

The real truth is … God isn't just with us when we're on top of everything. While life may bring us to the point of despair — and that shroud of melancholy and hopelessness may make us question whether or not God is present … we must remember that God is always present — in the valleys and on the hilltops! One writer put it this way, "God is closer than our next breath. The problem is with us. We just fail to notice the presence of God and need to look for God." God is not restricted to one location at a time. When we are in a crowd God is there. When we are alone, God is there with us. Here is how Paul, standing in the midst of the Areopagus, describes this truth: "For in him we live and move and have our being" *(Acts 17:28)*.

No, God doesn't promise to always lift us up and onto the hilltop, but God has promised that we are never without his presence, even when we are in the valley. God is there with us when the feeling of oppressiveness clouds our vision and when we feel as though we are a tattered, jumbled mess of frayed nerves. We are God's children. We are friends of Jesus and he promised to be with us always through the presence of the Holy Spirit.

So, here's my question for you: Where has God shown up where you have least expected it? When have you been in the valley, and yet God has somehow worked to turn it into something new, something good and full of grace? I have those places, and I know that in the midst of them I wondered where God was. And yet, looking back I now see how God could use even the hardest of situations to create something new, something better. Amen

CHAPTER SEVENTEEN

God Spoke To Job Out Of The Storm

"Then the LORD spoke to Job out of the storm." — Job 38:1, NIV

The story of Job is familiar to all of us. By the world's standards, Job of Uz was successful; by God's standards, he was righteous. You couldn't find a person who would say a bad word about Job. He was a wise man. And Job was a man whose public life was matched by his private piety. There was harmony in Job's family. His children all got along with each other. Furthermore, the biblical text underscores the fact that Job was just as righteous as he was rich and just as good as he was great. Above all he had respect for God and hated evil with a passion. Everything had gone well for Job until one day it all fell apart.

Job 1, verses 13-19 tell us all that happened to Job on one *Terrible, Horrible, No Good, Very Bad Day*. In one day, Job lost all his possessions, his financial portfolio, his children and the respect of his wife. One day he was wealthy and self-sufficient, and the next day he had nothing.

Soon after that first tragic day, Job lost his health. He was stricken with painful pus-filled, erupting sore boils from the soles of his feet to the crown of his head. He could not stand without standing on a boil. He could not sit without sitting on a boil. He could not lie down without lying on a boil.

We could go through this entire story and learn many lessons, but I want to focus our attention on when the Job saga took a drastic turn for the better. It is important to notice that for the first 37 chapters of the book of Job, his cries for God's help and relief were met only by God's deafening silence.

Have you ever been in a place where you felt God had abandoned you? If you have been a follower of Christ very long, you have had periods where it seems God is nowhere to be found. We often call them periods of spiritual dryness. Tragic events, unknown, incurable disease can cause even the stoutest Christian to ask: "If God is all powerful and he knows all things why did he allow this terrible thing happen to me?"

What do we do when we feel like God has forgotten us or our loved one? Sometimes what causes us the most pain and confusion isn't what God says to us but the fact that in the midst of difficulty God seems to say nothing at all.

Our ability to hang on is put to the test when a short-term experience becomes a long-term pattern. We feel like we can handle a short-term experience. We're not going to become hysterical over a mere "bump in the road." But sometimes a short-term bump in the road becomes a long-term pattern and we begin to wonder, "What is God doing? And why isn't God answering my prayers? Why isn't God helping me?" We wonder where God is when we are walking through the pain of divorce, or the crushing burden of having our friends turn on us, or the heartbreak of watching a loved one die. Even the Lord Jesus cried out from the Cross, "My God, my God, why have you forsaken me" *(Mark 15:34)*?

What do you do during the spiritually dry periods of life when it seems like God is doing nothing in your life? What are we to do when we don't hear God's voice? Here's what you do — you **trust God more… not less!** Times of silence — when our prayers seem to be unanswered, our requests seem to be rejected, our haters seem to be victorious, and our Omnipotent God seems to be quiet — may be filled with frustration and impatience, but ironically, those times when you don't hear God's voice on a particular issue require more faith. It may be that God is using that time for something bigger than you could have imagined… but whatever is next will most likely require a deeper level of trust.

For thirty-seven chapters Job was perplexed by his problems. He was questioning his quandary. Then, after all the weeks of silence, Job 38:1 says that God answered Job from out of the storm.

Now, in order for God to speak from out of the storm, God has got to be in the storm. And, that is the whole point of the Job narrative, bad things happen, and we don't know why, but God is there.

Yes, God had been silent a mighty long time. But, silence is not absence. Here Job sees, and we see, that even though God is sometimes silent, God is still present. If little else, Job teaches us that in the final analysis, we can trust the Lord our God. When God is silent and the strong winds are raging, we can still trust in the Lord. We can trust his mercy even when we can't trace his movements. We can trust his grace, even when we can't see his face.

Through the storm, Job found out that God is faithful. Even while the storm was tossing Job to-and-fro like a ragdoll, Job learned that God was still God and God was still present. God makes himself known, in the midst of Job's suffering. God answers Job out of the storm.

We don't always understand the cause of the storms, but they come into everyone's lives. No one is immune from them and when they hit they are unexpected, they are scary and they point to a God greater than ourselves.

God is in the storm to bring us through tragedy to triumph. He's in the storm to deliver us from grief to glory. He is there to transform our problems into praise. He's there to change our burdens into blessings. God is in the whirlwind to turn our tests into a testimony.

And that's when Job finally got in line for a mighty blessing. When Job accepted the fact that there are just some things in life that he would never understand; when he decided that he was just going to trust God and praise God and serve God, because of or in spite of his circumstances, that's when God gave Job twice as much as he had when he first started out. The Lord blessed the latter days of Job more than the first days of Job. And that same God will bless you!

CHAPTER EIGHTEEN

Quitters Don't Win Fights

"That is why we never give up. Though our bodies are dying, our spirits are being renewed every day."
— 2 Corinthians 4:16, NLT

On November 25th, 1980, Panamanian professional boxer Roberto Durán fought Ray Charles Leonard, better known as Sugar Ray Leonard, in what was billed as "The Super Fight," a boxing match which took place at the Louisiana Superdome in New Orleans in front of 25,038 fans. It was the second of three fights between the two.

The Durán-Leonard World Boxing Association Welterweight Championship fight became known as the *No Más* fight because in the closing seconds of the eighth round, Durán turned his back to Leonard and quit, saying to the referee *"No Más" (which translated in English means "No more")*. Afterwards, Sugar Ray Leonard said, "I *made* him quit. To make a man quit, to make Roberto Durán quit, was better than knocking him out."

Truth be told, there are times in the best of lives when the temptation to quit is overwhelming. Someone reading this chapter might be on the brink of walking away from responsibility *or* your family *or* your marriage *or* your job *or* life *or* God. You're trying to read your Bible more but the passion to do so hasn't materialized and reading your Bible is starting to feel like work. Relationships are draining you and although you'd never walk away, you are on the verge of checking out emotionally. We all hit a wall — a place where we feel like quitting because things get difficult or boring. The enormity of effort and the demands that keep pushing and pulling at us from every direction certainly can make us feel like quitting.

Think about this thought: we don't typically consider quitting until challenges and obstacles come our way. When we pursue a new relationship, career, craft or idea we usually always start with feelings of enthusiasm, hope and optimism. But, when an obstacle or challenge comes, it's then that we start to think about quitting.

The Apostle Paul states, in 2 Corinthians 4, verse 16, "That is why we never give up. Though our bodies are dying, our spirits are being renewed every day." The New Revised Version begins this same sentence: "So we do not lose heart."

What does it mean to "lose heart?" It means that you become so deeply discouraged that you lose courage — you lose confidence — you lose a sense of purpose — you give up ... quit ... throw in the towel ... you cry, "No más." And losing heart means you also gain some things. You gain a pessimistic attitude — you gain a demoralized attitude — you gain a defeated attitude — you gain a deflated spirit.

Think about this thought. **The thing people tend to forget when all they want to do is give up is that failure doesn't fix anything.** Whether you're trying to quit obsessing over social media or struggling to put an addiction behind you and turn over a new page; or whether you're trying to achieve a goal; the misery you were experiencing will be back, one way or another if you choose to give up at the most difficult time.

The question is when we feel like quitting ... how do we go on? What motivates us to continue? How can we say with Paul "We never give up?"

And this is the first thing I want you to remember. We continue. We persist. We prevail. We stick it out. We go on because of what we believe. Jesus said, in Mark 14, "If we can believe, all things are possible to us!"

Now think about this for a moment. God has no limitations! Our God can do anything, therefore, there is no person that God can't save. There is no sickness that God can't heal. There is no need that God can't meet. There is no place that God can't send revival. There is no situation that God can't turn around.

In 2 Corinthians 4:14, Paul quotes Psalm 116:10 when he says, "I believed, therefore I spoke..." Our words reveal what we believe, what we hold dear in our hearts. What you speak is evidence of your faith. Another way of saying that is: your speech reveals what you believe. Our words can either propel us though open doors or they can hold us back from walking into what God has prepared for us.

The gospelist Matthew quotes Jesus saying, "If you have faith, and do not doubt ... if you say to this mountain ... it shall happen" *(Matthew 21:21)*. For faith to operate, it must be released through spoken words, according to Jesus.

Faith is important because it affects our conduct; it affects our behavior, our words, and our witness. Firstly, when we believe God, our behavior is changed. Secondly, when a person by faith trust in the God Jesus knows and reveals her or his tongue is affected. Third, faith affects our witness. We can't be much of a witness for God if our faith is weak or nonexistent.

Many today are more inclined to believe the news media, their friends, as well as the many false philosophies of this world. In spite of this, God is the One Person that we need to believe above all others. God's Word is absolutely trustworthy. If there is one Person we can put our faith in, it is in God.

If you can believe, it is possible. If you can have faith for it, you can see it happen. Stay encouraged. Refuse to give up, in or out. Resolve to trust God!

CHAPTER NINETEEN

Picturing The Possible

¹¹ *So I came to Jerusalem and was there for three days.* ¹² *Then I got up during the night, I and a few men with me; I told no one what my God had put into my heart to do for Jerusalem. The only animal I took was the animal I rode.* ¹³ *I went out by night by the Valley Gate past the Dragon's Spring and to the Dung Gate, and I inspected the walls of Jerusalem that had been broken down and its gates that had been destroyed by fire.* ¹⁴ *Then I went on to the Fountain Gate and to the King's Pool; but there was no place for the animal I was riding to continue.* ¹⁵ *So I went up by way of the valley by night and inspected the wall. Then I turned back and entered by the Valley Gate, and so returned.* ¹⁶ *The officials did not know where I had gone or what I was doing; I had not yet told the Jews, the priests, the nobles, the officials, and the rest that were to do the work.* ¹⁷ *Then I said to them, "You see the trouble we are in, how Jerusalem lies in ruins with its gates burned. Come, let us rebuild the wall of Jerusalem, so that we may no longer suffer disgrace."* ¹⁸ *I told them that the hand of my God had been gracious upon*

me, and also the words that the king had spoken to me. Then they said, "Let us start building!" So they committed themselves to the common good. [19] But when Sanballat the Horonite and Tobiah the Ammonite official, and Geshem the Arab heard of it, they mocked and ridiculed us, saying, "What is this that you are doing? Are you rebelling against the king?" [20] Then I replied to them, "The God of heaven is the one who will give us success, and we his servants are going to start building; but you have no share or claim or historic right in Jerusalem."

— Nehemiah 2:11-20, NRSV

I researched this text and found that through it God's servant Nehemiah shows us how to be God's builders, how to bring about restoration in our lives, our homes, our Church, our community and the global village.

At the time we are introduced to Nehemiah he is serving as a cupbearer in Susa, the principal palace and winter residence of Artaxerxes, King of Persia. As a cupbearer, he is in a unique position. Back in the long ago, cupbearers were important and trusted servants of kings, not just as close advisors, but also because their responsibilities included preventing the king from being poisoned, whether accidentally, or as part of an assassination.

One day Nehemiah received a visit from his brother Hanani who reported that Jerusalem was in a blighted and deplorable condition. Nehemiah's heart was broken over the ruinous state of his people. Nehemiah's dismay was specifically directed toward the fact that the walls of the city remained broken down long after the Temple was destroyed. And his first response was to drop to his knees and pray.

In our text, Nehemiah shows us how to "picture the possible" before we take the next step whatever the next step might be. Let's look at Chapter 2:11-20.

The text begins with Nehemiah's words, "I went to Jerusalem." He says it matter-of-factly, as if he'd simply hopped in a car and driven up the street, when, in truth, he had traveled across fifteen hundred miles of searing desert, through hostile lands in response to God's call.

The point is this: whether we are building character, a family, a church, or a changed society, few things of lasting value are accomplished without our willingness to make a long, difficult journey. Even the nihilist, Frederick Nietzsche (born October 15, 1844 – died August 25, 1900) understood this truth when he said, "The essential thing in heaven and earth is that there should be a long obedience in the same direction; there thereby results, and has always resulted, in something which makes life worth living."

Sometimes we wander off the path. Sometimes we wonder if we can keep on keeping on — and sometimes we may even lose sight of God, who has called and is leading us. But the Bible makes clear that the power to bless and to build is given to those who go the distance.

In generic terms, think about what is required to enter into a meaningful relationship, a relationship that might last over the long term. You have to spend time together. You have to communicate, to share feelings and experiences. You have to share intimately. You have to commit to one another, so that you can trust one another when times are difficult.

God has committed to journey alongside us and support us through the roughest of times. Have we committed to following God even when it leads us into difficult paths? If you have not before, I encourage you to reimagine your life as a Jesus follower in these terms of discipleship; it's not about learning the rules of Christian behavior, but it is about entering into a relationship. Listen. Real, meaningful faith doesn't happen overnight ... it grows over time.

Our Sovereign Lord doesn't need any more groupies; he doesn't need any more spectators, eager for excitement but only in it for the ten-second sprint. What the Lord is looking for are people who are willing to enter into a real relationship with God and engagement in the breadth, depth and duration of God's love for the world every day, from now on. Christ doesn't need a larger crowd, ready to cheer and applaud louder and longer. What Jesus needs is a church — a community committed to serving God and one another, a model of loving, caring, committed relationship for all the world to see.

The apostle Paul put it this way: "Forgetting what lies behind and straining forward to what lies ahead, I press on toward the goal for the prize of the heavenly call of God in Christ Jesus" *(Philippians 3:13-14).*

Nehemiah said, "I went to Jerusalem." I have a question: How far are you willing to go for the Lord? for Justice?

These are severe days. When we solve one problem, another comes along. When we sit down to catch our breath from one struggle, a new one challenges us. When we put out one fire, a new one starts. Nehemiah was a member of a people who were denigrated and dismissed — like African Americans are today. A Rutgers University School of Criminal Justice study concluded that "in the U.S., African Americans are 2.5 times more likely to be killed by police than white people. For Black women, the rate is 1.4 times more likely." These are troubling times. We thought that things were going to get better. We thought that each generation was seeing progress, but instead we see an increasingly racialized society and one conspicuously more sinister than the world of yesterday. What must we do? How do we cope?

Notice what Nehemiah did. Verse 12 says, "I set out during the night with a few men. I had not told anyone what my God had put in my heart to do for Jerusalem." Nehemiah didn't begin his initiative under a spotlight, but in the dark of night. He didn't start by rallying mass involvement; he carefully selected a few people in whom to develop a vision. He didn't inaugurate his campaign by laying out his entire plan — instead, he sent his colleagues into the broken city and trusted that God would stir their hearts to action.

Sometimes when we look at things in such a state of disrepair, it's almost impossible to stay positive — unless we remember that God is in the picture! Unless we envision what is possible through God's gracious power and love.

In his ground-breaking book, *Experiencing God*, Henry Blackaby says that the chief problem confronting humanity today is not a lack of resources, but the lack of a God-sized vision. I believe this is true.

The writer of Proverbs says: "Where there is no vision, the people perish" *(Proverbs 29:18)*. But when God's vision is seen and spoken of; when people are willing to step out in faith and move towards God's vision, then anything is possible. I'm convinced that our families, workplaces, social circles and churches need all of us to be visionary leaders. And it won't be enough to speak of our vision. We must live it after the example of Jesus Christ, who cast a vision, not merely in words, but with his whole life.

As Nehemiah toured the ravaged city of Jerusalem, he saw nothing but hopeless destruction; burned out buildings and gates; the streets piled with rubbish heaps; people picking through the garbage to find something to eat. Their health and their hopes were haggard with relentless poverty.

He addressed those discouraged, apathetic people — not with a word of judgment, for they had been trying to rebuild for three years, but with a word of hope. He helped them picture the possibilities and offered an opportunity to DO something about their circumstances, saying, "Come, let us rebuild the wall of Jerusalem, and we will no longer be in disgrace. I also told them about the gracious hand of my God upon me."

Friends, Nehemiah reminds us that no matter how bad things look, builders never stop picturing what is possible when God shows up! God is "able to accomplish abundantly far more than all we can ask or imagine" *(Ephesians 3:20)*. Say that out loud: **God is**

able — to accomplish abundantly — far more — than all we can ask for — or imagine! God is able to rehabilitate your life! God is able to restore your relationships! God is able to renew the face of the earth! God is able to accomplish abundantly, far more than we can ask for or even imagine! Amen and hallelujah!

About the Author

Dr. Michael A. Bell has served as Senior Pastor-Resident Theologian of Greater St. Stephen First Church since July 1985. He is the first African American to be elected President of the Baptist General Convention of Texas *(BGCT)*, a convention of 5,700 churches, representing 2.5. million Baptists. Later, he was elected Chairman of Texas Baptist Committed, an organization formed to promote moderate principles and leadership within the BGCT. Dr. Bell also served two-terms as President of the African American Fellowship of Churches *(800+ churches)*. His denominational work includes serving on the Coordinating Council of the Cooperative Baptist Fellowship *(CBF)*. Additionally, he was appointed as Chairman of the CBF's Committee on Representation and Relationships. For a period, he was commissioned as International Dean for the Family Life International Fellowship. He is the first African American to be elected to the Mainstream Baptist Hall of Fame.

In the civic arena, Dr. Bell, a respected advocate for justice and equality, has served as Chairman of the Tarrant County American Cancer Society; Chairman and Co-Founder of Tarrant Clergy for Inter-Ethnic Peace and Justice; Chairman and Founder of the

Southeast Neighborhood Interest Coalition. He is co-founder of Unity in the Community Coalition — Fort Worth and presently serves as that consortium's facilitator. An educator and certified Life Coach, he has taught at Jarvis Christian College, Hawkins, Texas, in the capacity as Assistant professor of Religion. He is currently an Adjunct Professor at Brite Divinity School, Texas Christian University.

Dr. Bell is a graduate of Wiley College, Marshall, Texas *(Bachelor of Science)*; Howard University Divinity School, Washington, D.C. *(Master of Divinity)*; University of Texas at Tyler, Tyler, Texas *(Master of Arts)*; and Interdenominational Theological Center, Atlanta, Georgia *(Doctor of Ministry)*. He was a Howard Thurman Fellow while matriculating at Howard University Divinity School.

www.ingramcontent.com/pod-product-compliance
Lightning Source LLC
LaVergne TN
LVHW011956070526
838202LV00054B/4938